THROUGH THE
AGES

Kathryn Davis Henry

THROUGH THE
AGES

BY

KATHRYN DAVIS HENRY

THE PHILOSOPHICAL RESEARCH SOCIETY, INC.

Los Angeles, California

1988

ISBN No. 0-89314-423-1
L.C. 87-36607

The Philosophical Research Society acknowledges with gratitude
the donation by Kathryn Davis Henry of the
rights to and proceeds from the publication of this book.

Cover Illustration:
Southwest Amerindian petroglyphs in Gila Bend, Arizona. Photos by Abby Kennedy.

Library of Congress Cataloging in Publication Data
Henry, Kathryn Davis, 1918-
    Symbolism through the ages / by Kathryn Davis Henry.
        p.   cm.
    Bibliography: p.
    ISBN 0-89314-423-1
    1. Symbolism.   2. Signs and symbols.   3. Title.
BL600.H42 1988   87-36607
001.51—dc19   CIP

Published by
THE PHILOSOPHICAL RESEARCH SOCIETY, INC.
3910 Los Feliz Boulevard, Los Angeles, CA 90027
Printed in the U.S.A.

*Dedicated with gratitude
to my teacher,
MANLY P. HALL*

TABLE OF CONTENTS

Note: Illustrations follow their subject chapter.

FOREWORD

Symbolism is a universal language, indispensable to the perpetuation of knowledge and permitting us to experience the unfoldment of our own mental powers. Early history has descended to us through glyphs, designs, images, and petroglyphs, some of which are no longer explainable. There is no area of exact science in which strange devices and mysterious designs are not still in common use. Magical emblems were drawn on rocks, carved into wood, or traced on sheets of papyrus. Many ancient peoples had protective charms with strange inscriptions, to be worn on persons or displayed on the walls of homes to protect the human soul from spiritual contamination.

From the distant monasteries of Tibet to the great churches and cathedrals of Europe, spiritual truths have been communicated by various artistic media including painting, music, and architecture. Even today secular organizations proclaim their identities by logos which appear on their letterheads or their products. We take it all for granted, and in so doing have deprived ourselves of a world of wonders and a more intimate contact with the divine powers that govern all things.

From the beginning the sacred mysteries of existence could not be communicated by means ordinarily available to the profane. The Divine Presence manifests through an infinite variety of symbolic devices. Every form in nature is an expression of the universal energy which sustains all. What this energy is we do not know, it cannot be seen, but we become aware of it through the forms in which its principles are clothed. Every religion has developed a language of symbolism—a variety of sacred emblems, myths, legends, and artistries in order that believers can be more easily convinced of the reality of things unseen. There are many unsolved mysteries which still plague all fields of knowledge and the proper solutions may lie in the correct interpretation of crude figures and devices which have descended to us from the remote past.

For many years my good friend Kathryn Davis Henry has researched among artistic relics of antiquity for those artifacts which bear witness to the noble quest of all ages for the meaning of existence. Her notes and commentaries make a valid contribution to the illustrations which she has assembled. This labor of love testifies to a lifelong dedication to the advancement of knowledge and understanding.

Mrs. Henry has gathered here an extraordinary group of symbols derived from many parts of the world over a long period of time. Symbols communicate. They are valuable to the archaeologist because through them he can participate with antiquity rather than merely reflect upon ancient ways. To the artist they are significant shorthand elements of identification. In Christian theology saints were represented by the instruments of their martyrdom, and the Eastern sages by devices which explain their attributes, or the benefits which they can bestow upon mankind. All things visible are masks concealing invisible powers and principles. Our own faces, attitudes, and mannerisms tell something about ourselves, and what the oriental calls "the mirror of gestures" makes communion of souls possible.

We learn from psychology that in the process of visualization we see more than we realize, and the subconscious can often explain to us what the conscious has never known. This elaborate book of symbols presents an adventure bearing witness to the eternal search for the purpose of life. Most of all, sacred symbolism not only reveals meaning, but comforts us with the realization that symbols signify the promise of the ultimate truths we are all seeking.

We congratulate Mrs. Henry for the insights which she gives us through her studies of symbolism. It should be of value to all truthseekers everywhere and a handy reference work for students of comparative religion and the esoteric arts and sciences.

Manly P. Hall

INTRODUCTION

My interest in symbolism was stimulated when a teacher of philosophy, Charles Robert Wilson, told me about a section of bas-relief sculpture which was, at that time, in the Museum of Natural History (Field Museum) in Chicago.

The sculpture was executed during the time of the rise of the ancient Maya civilization in Central America. It showed an elephant of the kind that was brought from Asia to this continent in more recent times. At the time when the bas-relief was made, there were no elephants of that type on this continent!

There were mastodons and mammoths on the North American continent, but they were of a different structure from the elephant of Asia which is so familiar to us today. The American mastodon is extinct and extended from the Oligocene to the late Pleistocene age. Remains of the mammoth have been found in Pleistocene deposits. The Imperial Mammoth of the American Pleistocene stood fourteen feet high with long, upward curving tusks.

There was not only contact between the Maya and the Asiatics (the two continents), but also a deep relationship or knowledge of Oriental customs by the Maya since the elephant in Asia is a religious symbol signifying the attributes of wisdom, royalty and generosity. I have found many elephant symbols in varying cultures. All ancient civilizations used art as a medium through which to express great truths in symbolic form. While the majority of the works of art were of a sacred nature in antiquity, there are artworks depicting everyday life. Some of these were funerary, carved on sarcophagii indicating the trades or positions held during the lives of the individuals. There were also public works showing chariot races and gladiator events as in Rome. Wars and hunts were carved in bas-relief and painted in various civilizations, but these were often symbolic and allegorical as well as historical.

In antiquity, the inner sanctum of the priesthoods (of the mystery schools which preceded the theologians) wrote in allegorical and symbolic form to deliberately conceal great truths from the masses. This was done in order to protect the Great World Teachings from falling into the wrong hands. The priests were fearful that great knowledge would be used the wrong way and thus become extremely dangerous. This method, concealed to the profane yet revealed to those of enlightenment, proved to be an excellent method of teaching. "In the beginning was the Word" teaches the evolvement of creation, long before biblical times. The Great Teachings can mainly be articulated and understood by way of symbol, analogy and parable.

In the religions and philosophies, great truths were woven into symbolism. Even historical peoples and places had myths woven around them. Throughout generations these truths have been displayed as magnificently beautiful, sacred works of art. We hope to be able to show the images and meanings of these sacred symbols. Instead of perpetuating the differences we will try to explain the similarities of sacred symbols, which are traceable through the spiritual arts of the ages, and attempt to discover the reasons for the symbology. In all religions there are paradises, God and/or gods, divine souls, teachers, world virgins, halos, saviors, trinities, angels, and a host of other identities. Dates and eras are not pertinent to the subject.

In some ancient cultures there was monotheism as in Judaism, and one hundred years before in the Egyptian reign of Ahknaton. In some there were pantheons. Where there was more than one god, it was all the same essence of the Godhead, but divided into separate powers such as in Neo-Platonism; everywhere we find unity in division and division in unity.

Universal law was taught by the use of and explained by allegories, mythologies and symbologies of various philosophies and religions, and from the msytery schools throughout the passing of time. Many of these symbols used by the mystery schools and others came out of the collective unconscious of the human life-wave. This was explained beautifully by Dr. Carl Jung, famous Swiss psychologist. As time went on, superstition often resulted because of these concepts being interpreted as literal and historical. When the great and beautiful meanings behind the symbolism are realized, it is as though the door is opened—revealing the whole room instead of just a glimpse through the keyhole. No one religion is greater than another. Whenever these mythological concepts are taken as historical fact, not only does superstition and the wrong use of God's energy prevail, but ritualism also replaces the search for ultimate truth.

Focusing on particulars, in animal symbolism there are all of the cat family (the feline species), bulls, dogs, deer, elephants, fish, lambs and rams, snakes, crocodiles, and rabbits. Then there are the mythological creatures of many different civilizations: phoenix birds, griffins, winged horses, unicorns, centaurs, minotaurs, harpies, three-headed dogs, and others.

In nearly all the seven great world religions there are flowers, rivers, trees, birds, insects, serpents, trinities, fruit, stars, crosses, and similar feast days. The meanings behind these symbols, allegories and myths are far more wonderful and beautiful than when they are perceived as literal and historical figures. In the various religions and philosophies, all religious symbols have been taken from universal law, but as the truth of the law has been passed down through the ages, man has misinterpreted, mistranslated, misunderstood, misused, and abused. Each group of religions declares that only through their particular method can an individual be saved or reach the higher realms. Man in his evolvement, however, must function on different levels of understanding in all the various facets and departments of life; in the physical, mental and emotional planes.

It is the hope of the author that this work will help to create more tolerance and understanding for the beliefs and faiths of others, and awareness that the same stream of divine energy flows through us all, throughout our world and the universe.

THE FISH AND FLOOD LEGENDS

THE FISH

Manly Hall, author and director of the Philosophical Research Society, Inc., observed that in the Brahmanic Mysteries of India, the Universe was born from the womb of the deity Meru, according to allegory of old traditions, and the incarnations of Vishnu follow the months of the prenatal period of the human embryo, his nine appearances closely paralleling the nine principal changes taking place in the human embryo previous to birth. The Egg of Brahma is the story of the cosmic embryo, and embryology is the basic study of creation. In this law of analogy, the great Lord Vishnu has already come nine times into the world to save his people. His tenth is yet to come. Five other civilizations have used the Egg symbol of creation.

Vishnu was first born out of the mouth of a Fish. He then rose out of the body of a Turtle. Still later he appeared as a Boar, then a Lion, afterwards as a Monkey, and, after a number of other changes, he appeared as (dwarfed) man. Mr. Hall recalls that some time ago a scientist had arranged a table showing the relationship of the human being to various animals during the prenatal period. He followed exactly the list of incarnations of Vishnu, while totally unaware that he was linking together Oriental occultism and Occidental embryology. (For the purpose of emphasis, I have capitalized all symbols. Because of my great respect for Manly Palmer Hall, I do not refer to him merely as "Hall.")

Signs of Life by H. M. Raphaelian (and Manly Hall in his work) shows Oannes, Babylonian god of science, wearing a Fish headdress reminiscent of ribbon-tailed bilurcated mitres of leaders of Christianity. Manly Hall, in his *Secret Teachings of All Ages,* shows Oannes as a Fish, also. The Fish became the sign of believers in Christ among early Christians, and the Savior's monogram was designed from the Greek word "itchthys," meaning Fish. The Fish pertains to Christ, whose first apostles were Fishermen (Fishers of Men) and subject to miraculous draughts and multiplication of Fish. Those who were caught in the net of his word, or Truth, became the faithful, saved from sin (by living the pure life), and were baptized in water. Water is the symbol of the "Living Waters," to be mentioned again, which bestowed the spiritual ecstasy that came from God's energy.

The Fish is the symbol of the spiritual food and is also the symbol of the astrological sign of Pisces. The sign has many key words, particularly being known for the elements of emotion and mysticism. The fish is said to have had an important part in identifying Christians to each other in times of persecution, drawing pictures of it in the earth with their feet for the purpose of recognizing each other in secret. Prophets are born under this sign.

In the paired fish of the Oriental "Li," Raphaelian says there is a relation to the general and universal symbolic idea of the Fish which is love, union and the providence of God and also of opposite polarities, that of rising to the top or descending to self-undoing.

1

In *Mythology and the Bible* the late Corinne Heline describes Perseus, in Greek mythology, as spending three days in the body of a monster, paralleling the story of Jonah and the whale in the Bible. She relates another parallel, the story of the Greek Hercules who kills a great sea monster by leaping fully armed into its throat and fighting for three days in its belly before coming forth victorious!

In ancient Hebrew, the word "jonah" (not a proper name) means Dove, initiate or prophet. The Fish signifies hidden truth, and a ship represents the soul on the sea of life. This is an allegory of the Piscean Age of the Fish. The Fish lives hidden in the deep, and early Christians had to keep their faith hidden.

In Peter Lum's book, *Fabulous Beasts,* he writes about Ea, god of ocean and subeterranean streams, the great water-god of the Babylonians, saying that on a Babylonian seal stone of the Eighteenth Century B.C., Ea is pictured standing on a goat-fish and on a mermaid.

The goat-fish is really the combination of two astrological symbols, Capricorn and Saturn symbolized by the Goat combined with Pisces and Neptune symbolized by the Fish and equalling a great world teacher. The Goat often has a Fish tail in this symbol.

Peter Lum in *Fabulous Beasts* said that Ea lived in the depths of the sea and that he was highly evolved with supreme intelligence, knowing all things. He came ashore every morning, accepting no food on land, and then he would return to the sea in the evening. He taught the people all the arts and sciences, how to write with a stylus on clay tablets, gave them laws, and taught them how to build houses and temples. He told them of the gods who dwelt in the land from whence he had come.

There is another description of Ea that Manly Hall, Lum, Heline, and Raphaelian all narrate: a human being from the waist up, but like a Fish from the waist down. Lum says it was really Ea, under the name of Oannes, in that particular allegory.

Lum continues to say that mermaids and mermen held vases of life-giving water belonging to Ea, the water-god. The "Living Waters," the elixir of life, is the essence of energy and not liquid at all. Lum said there were tales of Fish gods from other parts of the world but none having the stature of Ea. They are usually bringers of culture and protection to mankind. He tells about the Polynesian Vat*ea*, who was considered the father of gods and men and who was half human and half Porpoise in form.

The North American Indians, according to Lum, tell a story of having once lived in a land far away to the west on a barren coastland. They did not know how to find food and were hungry and cold. Then a man arose from the sea and came close to shore but did not touch the land. He looked like a man from the waist up, but he had two fishtails for legs, and although his face seemed to have been human, it resembled that of a Porpoise. He had long green hair and beard, and as he floated on the water, he would sing to the people and tell them about the beautiful land of the sea from which he had come that had treasures and strange Fish people and a lovely green light that shown in deep waters. The people were frightened because they knew that those who disappeared under the water never returned. Then he told them that he could guide them to a land across the waters where they could find food and live. (In Egypt, Osiris, god of the Nile, is usually pictured in a green color.)

Although at first the Indians were fearful and hesitated, they decided to trust the Fish Man since they were starving and cold. This is the story of why the Indians came from Asia to North America. The Fish Man or Fish God then disappeared as he sang, never to be seen again. (There is a picture of the North American Indian Fish Man in a museum in Boulder, Colorado.) This deity, according to Mr. Lum's narration, was most friendly to mankind (as were all the great world teachers) and saved the earth from complete destruction.

Lum explained how we know today of this particular Fish legend. It was preserved in the writings of one of the fathers of the church who had copied it from a late manuscript of a Babylonian priest. The legend tells of great numbers of people of diverse origin who gathered in Babylon and lived in orderless confusion. From out of the Erythrean Sea appeared Oannes of great intelligence, having the body of a Fish. A human head had grown under the Fish head and feet under the tail. He also spoke with a human voice.

One day I was reading a children's book to a little child. The story was taken in exact content from the religious allegory that Peter Lum told about. As to the allegory Lum said that, according to the East Indians, the God Vishnu took the form of a Fish to save Manu from the great Flood. While performing his morning ablutions, Manu, a sage and virtuous man (like his counterpart Noah), found a tiny Fish in the river next to which he was standing. Just as he was about to throw the Fish back into the water, it spoke to him. It begged him not to leave it in the water until it had grown bigger because the great creatures of the sea frightened him. Manu, therefore, put it into a bowl, but by morning the Fish had grown so large that the bowl was too small, and eventually it would grow too large for the largest cauldron and even too large for a lake.

Finally Manu was able to get the enormous Fish to the sea. The Fish spoke to him, telling him that in Seven days there would be a great Flood. The Fish said it would send a Ship for him and the Seven Sages and told him to take two of every creature from the earth and air and the seeds of every plant with them in this Ship. The Fish, you remember, was actually the God Vishnu.

Manu did as he was told, and the sea flowed over the earth as the promised great Ship appeared. Vishnu in his Fish shape guided the Ship with all on-board. The Fish was huge and with golden scales (like the sacred golden Carp of the Japanese) fastened the Ship to his single horn (like the Unicorn) and towed it up to the peak of the great Mountains to the north. As the waters began to subside, Manu was able to gradually guide the Ship down the Mountain slope and back to his land. Since that time the Mountain has borne the name "The Descent of Manu." From the book of Genesis, some believe this to be the counterpart of Mt. Ararat and the Ark (man).

Manly Hall, in his *The Secret Teachings of All Ages,* shows the Ark encompassing Noah, who is lying prone, and the Ark having man's measurements in its construction. He also shows a picture of Oannes, the Fish Man. He said that Berossus describes Oannes as follows: "At Babylon there was a great resort of people of various nations, who inhabited Chaldea and lived in a lawless manner like the beasts of the field." Here is another account of the same allegory.

"In the first year, there appeared from that part of the Erythrean Sea, which borders upon Babylonia, an animal destitute of reason, by name, Oannes, whose whole body, according to the account of Appollodorus, was that of a Fish; that under the Fish's head, he had another head, with feet also below, similar to those of a man, subjoined to the Fish's tail. His voice, too, and language was articulate and human; and a representation of him is preserved even to this day. This being was accustomed to passing the day among men but took no food at that season; and he gave them an insight into letters and sciences, and arts of every kind. He taught them to construct cities, to found temples, to compile laws, and explained to them the principles of geometric knowledge. He made them distinguish the seeds of the earth and showed them how to collect the fruits; in short, he instructed them in everything which could tend to soften manners and humanize their lives. From that time, nothing material has been added by way of improvement to his instructions. When the Sun had set, this being, Oannes, retired again into the sea and passed the night in the deep, for he was amphibious. After this there appeared other animals like Oannes. . . ." There is more on this subject from *Ancient Fragments* by Isaac Preston Cory.

Manly Hall said that every existing creature manifests some aspect of the intelligence or power of the Eternal One, who can never be known save through a study and appreciation of his numbered but inconceivable parts. When a creature is chosen, therefore, to symbolize the concrete human mind, in some concealed abstract principle, it is because its characteristics demonstrate the invisible principle in visible action. Fishes, insects, animals, reptiles, and birds appear in the religious symbolism of nearly all nations, because the forms and habits of those creatures and the media in which they exist closely relate them to the various generative and germinative powers of nature . . . evidence of divine omnipresence.

I quote from Manly Hall: "The early philosophers and scientists, realizing that all life has its origin in water, chose the Fish as the symbol of the life germ. The fact that Fishes are so prolific, makes the simile still more apt. While the early priests may not have possessed the instruments necessary to analyze the spermatazoan, they concluded by deduction that it resembled a fish."

"Fishes were sacred to the Greeks and Romans being connected with the worship of Aphrodite (Venus)." Manly Hall added, "An interesting survival of pagan ritualism is found in the custom of eating fish on Friday. Freya, in whose honor the day was named, was the Scandinavian Venus, and this day was sacred among many nations to the goddess of beauty and fecundity. This analogy further links the Fish with the procreative mystery. Friday is also sacred to the followers of Mohammed."

The word "nun" means both fish and growth, and as Inman says: "The Jews were led to victory by the Son of the Fish, whose other names were Joshua and Jesus (the Savior)."

4

Nun is still the name of a devotee of the Christian faith, Manly Hall says, and "among early Christians, three Fishes were used to signify the Trinity, and the Fish is also one of the eight sacred symbols of the great Buddha. It is also significant that the dolphin be sacred to both Apollo (the solar Savior) and Neptune. The dolphin was accepted by the early Christians as an emblem of Christ, because the pagans had viewed this beautiful creature as a friend and benefactor to man and the symbol of the divine preservative power. The first advocates of Christianity likened converts to Fishes, who at the time of baptism, 'returned again into the sea of Christ.'"

Manly Hall adds: "Among the Chinese the Fish typified contentment and good fortune and Fishes appeared on many of their coins. When used as a symbol of evil, the Fish represented the earth (man's lower nature) and the tomb (sepulchre of the Mysteries). Thus was Jonah in the belly of the 'Great Fish,' as Christ was three days in the tomb."

"The story of Jonah is really a legend of initiation into the Mysteries, and the 'Great Fish' represents the darkness of ignorance which engulfs man when he is thrown over the side of the Ship (is born) into the Sea (of Life). More probably the 'Whale' of Jonah is based upon the pagan mythological creature, Hypocampus, part horse and part dolphin, for the early Christian statues and carvings show the composite creature and not a true Whale."

"It is reasonable to suppose that the mysterious sea Serpents, which according to the Maya and Toltec legends brought the gods to Mexico, were Viking or Chaldean ships, built in the shape of composite sea monsters or Dragons. According to many scattered fragments extant, man's lower nature was symbolized by a tremendous awkward creature resembling a great sea Serpent or Dragon, called Leviathon. All symbols having serpentine form or motion signify the solar energy in one of its many forms. This great creature of the sea, therefore, represents the solar life force imprisoned in water and also the divine energy coursing through the body of man, where, until transmuted, manifests itself as a writhing, twisting monster; representing man's greeds, passions and lusts ."

In astrology, Manly Hall describes the constellation of Capricorn (similarly to other authors), "in which the winter solstice theoretically takes place, was called the House of Death, for in winter all life in the Northern Hemisphere is at its lowest ebb. Capricorn is a composite creature, with the head and upper body of a Goat and the tail of a Fish. . . . During the Age of Pisces, the Fish was the symbol of Divinity and the Sun god fed the multitude with two small Fishes. The front-piece of Inman's *Ancient Faiths* shows the Goddess Isis (Egyptian) with a Fish on her head." This is also pictured in H. W. Raphaelian's *Signs of Life*. Manly Hall said that the Indian (Hindu) Savior, Christna, in one of his incarnations, was cast from the mouth of a Fish!

Not only is Jesus often referred to as the Fisher of Men, but John Lundy said that the word "Fish" is an abbreviation of the whole title, Jesus Christ, Son of God, Savior and Cross. St. Augustine expressed that if you join together the initial letters of the five Greek words, *Inoous Xploros Otovru'os Ewtn'p,* which means Jesus Christ, Son of God, Savior, they make the word IXORE, meaning "Fish." It is this symbol in which "Christ is mystical-

5

ly understood because he was able to live in the abyss of this morality, as in the depth of waters." That is, without sin, as Manly Hall expressed it. Prophets, great world teachers and saviors are said to have been born under the sign of Pisces the Fish. Many Christians observe Friday, which is sacred to the Virgin (Venus), as a day upon which they shall eat Fish, not meat, as previously observed.

Besides the Fish Man of Babylonia, Persia, Maya, and Chaldea, there was the Fish Man of the Figi Islands. The Alaskan Indian had an allegory also of the Thunderbird and steel-headed man who changed into a steel-headed salmon. The Fish is the symbol of spiritual food.

There is a reed boat in the form of a monstrous Shark with a woman tied within it found in a drawing from Peru that is not unlike the Fish boat of Dionysus from the Grecian allegory.

FLOOD LEGENDS

In *The Stars in Myth and Fact*, Oral Scott tells of the activity of the Pleiades at the time of one of the great Floods which folk songs and stele have told about in the legends of many nations; of the sinkings of a mother civilization, Atlantis, and the rising of other continents and islands.

From "Kumulipo," a chant of creation about Hawaii's volcanic origin from *Hawaii Volcanoes* by Glen Kaye, the early Hawaiians talked about when the earth became hot, the heavens turned about, the Sun was darkened, the Moon shone, and the Pleiades (a star cluster) rose, and there was slime which became the source of the earth.

Noah (being a word for prophet in ancient Hebrew) is personified and woven into a beautifully veiled allegory in the Bible. The great Floods were historical, but allegories were woven around them for instruction purposes.

Dr. Thomas A. King in his *Allegories of Genesis* asks questions. He wonders if it is reasonable to suppose that Noah, with the primitive tools and limited materials at his disposal, could build a seaworthy Ark of the dimensions recorded in the Biblical account of the Flood. He wonders about the problem of ventilation, which would have been insurmountable with only one small window eighteen inches square.

According to Robert Graves, Greek mythology tells about the Flood. In *Deucolions Flood*, Graves relates the symbology of the Ark. The Dove and the Mountain are in the Greek story.

The Great Flood of the Bible (Genesis, Old Testament) is recorded by many ancient civilizations:

1. The Egyptians on papyrus told of their ancestral cultural heritage coming from people who had lived on islands to the west of them at the time of the Flood.

2. The North, Central (Maya and Aztec) and South American Indians (Inca) had Flood legends telling of their ancestral cultural heritage having been given to them by people from islands to the east, at the time of the Flood.

3. In ancient Greece, Plato, the great philosopher, had an ancestor, Solon (600 B.C.), who passed the Flood information on to him from the priests of Sais, who read of it from hieroglyphics recorded on stone pillars.

4. The Druids had feast days in honor of the dead from the sinkings.

5. The Persians had Flood legends.

6. The Mexican story of Noah, which came from pre-Columbian times, the Maya civilization.

7. Natives of the Caribbean islands have records of the Floods.

8. Flood legends are in Chinese mythology.

9. Recorded Flood legends by the Chaldeans.

10. Scandinavian legends of the Floods.

11. Polynesian legends of the Floods.

12. The Scottish Feast of the Candles honors the Flood dead.

13. The Japanese Feast of the Lanterns honors the Flood dead, also.

14. All Saints Day (Christian) honors the many who died and is depicted today by Halloween, the Hallowed Eve.

Ivory Netsuke

Sketch by K.H.

An Oriental teacher rides a giant Fish (Carp). The tail of the
Fish curls up over the head of the scholar as with the Naga
of India over the head of Krishna. The Fish has a horn like
the Unicorn. The golden Carp is very highly revered in Japan.

K.H.

INDIA
Fish incarnation of Vishnu found in *Asiatic
Mythology* by J. Haiken and *Man, The Grand
Symbol* by Manly P. Hall.

8

Outline portion sketch
K.H.

JAPAN
The Goddess Kwannon rides the giant Sacred Carp. By Hokusai, famous Japanese artist.

THE FISH

Original drawing by K.H. after the style of Hokusai of Japan. Fish is a sacred symbol in many ancient civilizations.

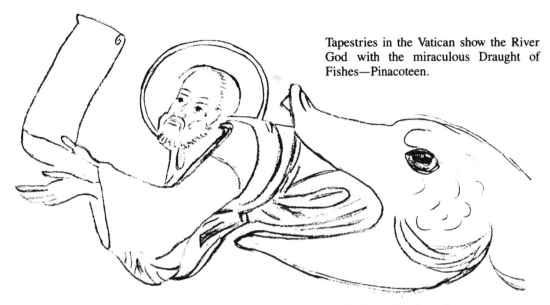

Tapestries in the Vatican show the River God with the miraculous Draught of Fishes—Pinacoteen.

Jonah emerging from the mouth of a Fish (not a Whale), after three days.
Outline from Monastery of Sumela, Trabzon, Turkey.

Fish by Marjean Von Engeln.

11

Sketch by K.H.

PHILISTINE

Dagon, the Fish-God. His chief temples were at Gaza and Ashdod.
From an old Bible combined with its own encyclopedia. Miss Fanny Cor-
beaux *(The Rephaim)* shows that the Chaldean *Oannes,* the Egyptian *On*
and the Philistine *Dagon* are identical in name and nature. This god was
also known in Assyria. *Derketo* was the female (as Dagon was the male),
and was worshipped at Ashkelon. She had a woman's face and a fish-body.
Atergatis, Argatis, Arathis and Argata are different forms of Derketo.

12

THE BULL AND OTHER ANIMALS

THE BULL

This interesting symbol, the Bull, was originally featured in cosmic myths, in the ceremonies of the mystery schools of antiquity, and was referred to in connection with the vernal equinox and the constellation of Taurus the Bull. Oral E. Scott in his book, *The Stars in Myth and Fact,* said that Taurus is the Bull which 4,000 years ago was the leader of the zodiac. In the present era it is Aries, the Ram or Lamb, which is the leader of the star group. In the ancient sacred art of various countries, the Bull is sometimes shown as goring the enemy. Every zodiacal sign has its ruling planet, and Venus is the planet ruling Taurus which has its higher and lower elements. The Bull, shown breaking the Auric Egg for new life to appear at the time of the vernal equinox (spring season), gives a reflection of universal rebirth to earth. It is this symbol of the heavens that was revered at that time by those of fine mind and character of the mystery schools. This symbol has been carried down into the legends of many civilizations.

Before the days of Abraham, Taurus led the starry procession, and the Bull was honored as the leader of the heavenly hosts. Scott said that in Egypt the Bull was worshipped under the name of Apis and was identified with Osiris, the Bull-god and god of the Nile. Rivers represent the spine or Ladder of soul development in various ancient religions which we will discuss later. Serapis is a combination of the gods Osiris and Apis and an interesting factor in this pantheon.

Continuing again with Scott, he mentions that the Bull in ancient Akkadia was the Bull of Light, and in Persia was worshipped as the symbol of re-creation. The Bull was held sacred by the Druids, who observed a great festival in his honor on the first day of May; the present celebration of May Day is a survival of this old Taurus festival. The May Pole is phallic, pertaining to creation.

Scott said that the Scottish people have traditions concerning the sacred Candlemas Bull who, it is said, is seen rising in the twilight of New Year's Eve and sailing across the sky. Thus is the Feast of the Candles.

Scott relates that this constellation, rich in myth and legend, comes from many lands and from many ancient sources. It is the Greeks, he says, to whom we are indebted for the most complete mythology. He concedes this was the Cretan Bull vanquished by Hercules and also the Bull battled by Jason, who is pictured in the sky as Orion, his club raised over the constellation of Taurus. He says that this was also the white Bull that bore Europa over the seas to the continent which now bears her name.

Scott tells the story that Europa was the daughter of Aganor, King of Phoenicia, and, Europa being very beautiful, Jupiter (Zeus) fell in love with her. He changed himself into a snow white Bull, mingling with her father's herds in order not to frighten her. So gentle was the Bull that Europa caressed him and put garlands around his neck, then climbed upon his back. Jupiter took advantage of the situation and moved quietly toward the beach. Then he plunged into the sea and swam to the island of Crete. Scott relates further in the allegory that upon their arrival at the island, Jupiter revealed himself to Europa and won her for his bride.

Tennyson writes about "The Wild Bull's Golden Horn" and of the star group, the Pleiades (a group of suns), within the constellation of Taurus, from which many Flood legends have come. He describes them as a "Glitter like a swarm of fire flies tangled in a silver braid."

In Crete, at the Palace of Knossos of the Minoan civilization, there was a strange practice called "bull-dancing." The mystery of this "bull-vaulting" could have been a ceremonial exercise. Greek mythology seems to verify this, and in Homer's *Iliad* is mentioned the delight of the earth-shaker god in Bulls, according to Scott. Manly Hall also concedes to the idea that the acrobatic bull-jumping is a sacred ceremony. It is a fascinating experience to visit the palace and see the well-known frescoes at Knossos. On the palace grounds are huge bull horns called the "horns of consecration," and there is a red-columned porch called the "Bull Portico."

The four great fixed constellations, Taurus (Bull), Leo (Lion), Scorpio (Serpent, Eagle, Dove), and Aquarius (Man or Cherub), are the symbols of Matthew, Mark, Luke and John. Manly Hall said they were the mysterious composites which formed the sphinxes and phoenixes of ancient legends and mythology. He added that they represented the four great points of the heavens. The four seasons, the two solstices and the two equinoxes which are connected across the circle by two lines, form a Cross within that circle. This is the symbol of our earth, and we will discuss the Cross symbol further along; this is one of many symbols which has been found all over our planet in various eras of time.

The Egyptian sacred Bull or Apis was also the symbol of the Sun at the vernal equinox and an emblem of the element earth. Hathor, the cow goddess of Egypt, may have been not just a fertility goddess, but one of creation. Manly Hall said that the Bull represented also the animal nature of man and for this reason was sacrificed upon the altars of such mysteries as the Jewish and Druids. Plutarch wrote that "The Apis (Bull) ought ever to be regarded by us as a fair and beautiful image as the soul of Osiris; Osiris who represents the spiritual nature of the lower world who is murdered and distributed throughout the substance of the physical spheres; the Apis is the emblem of the material world within which is the spiritual nature—Osiris. The Apis is also the symbol of the exoteric (or profane) doctrine, in contradiction to the esoteric (or divine) teachings represented by the uraeus worn upon the foreheads of the priests. From this is derived the mythological allegory of Serapis, who in a certain sense is not only the composite figure of Osiris and the lower world, in which he is incarnated, but also of the Mysteries, which are the terrestrial bodies containing the secret teachings or the spiritual soul."

The worship of the Bull in the ancient world was, in India, the white Bull of Siva (but the meaning is not understood today as it was in the past). The Bull symbol was also venerated in Persia, Chaldea, Phoenicia, Assyria, and Greece. Manly Hall states that the Bull was a phallic emblem signifying the paternal creative power of the Demiurgus in Egyptian and Hindu symbology. (Its use became a misuse of the interpretation of the symbol.) In his book, *The Secret Teachings of All Ages,* Manly Hall shows the Bembime Tablets of Isis where an individual is holding up the phallic symbol of the Bull. He says that "As the sign rising over the horizon at the vernal equinox constitutes the starry body for the annual incarnation of the Sun, the Bull not only was the celestial symbol of the Solar Man, but because the vernal equinox took place in the constellation of Taurus, it was called the 'breaker' or 'opener' of the year. The Apis further signifies that the God-mind is incarnated in the body of a beast and therefore that physical beast form is the sacred vehicle of divinity. Thus, man's lower personality is the Apis in which Osiris incarnates."

This is reminiscent, I believe, of St. Paul's version of the Christ (consciousness) within, the hope and glory, the Buddhic consciousness of the Oriental, the Daemon within of Socrates and the early Greeks, and the Nam of the Hindu. Man's higher self is within the lower vehicle, the physical body.

Mr. Hall said that, in regard to the soul and the physical body, the result of the combination is the creation of Sor-Apis (Serapis)—the material soul as ruler of the irrational material body and involved therein. After a certain period, which is determined by the square of five or 25 years, the body of the Apis is destroyed and the soul liberated by the water which drowns the material life. The Apis was taken to the Nile or a fountain and drowned at age 25, and there was mourning until a new Apis was found and Osiris was reincarnated with much rejoicing (a ceremony derived out of a deep meaning allegory and used in other religions, some following the early Egyptian).

This was indicative of the washing away of the material nature by the baptismal waters of divine light and truth, like the living waters of Christianity that followed. Mr. Hall describes the drowning of the Apis as the symbol of death, the resurrection of Osiris in the new Bull as the symbol of eternal renovation. The white Bull was symbolically sacred as the appointed emblem of the initiates, signifying the spiritualized material bodies of both man and nature.

In all Oriental symbolism the dagger and sword were symbolically used to cut away the bonds of materiality, severing it from the spiritual. In Christianity it is the spear which pierces the place where the seed atom of the lower emotional nature is located (around the liver area of the physical body). More on this aspect later.

Mr. Hall also said that in antiquity it was decreed that when the vernal equinox no longer occurred in the sign of Taurus, the Sun god incarnated in the sign of Aries and the Ram then became the vehicle of the solar power. Thus, the Sun rising in the sign of the celestial Lamb triumphs over the symbolic Serpent of darkness. We will speak further on Serpent symbolism as we come to it later in the book. He also said that the Lamb is a familiar emblem of purity because of its gentleness and the whiteness of its wool, and in many of the pagan mysteries it signified the universal Savior; in Christianity it is the favorite symbol of Christ. He mentioned that early church paintings show a Lamb standing upon a little hill, and from its feet pour four streams of living water signifying the four Gospels. The blood of the Lamb, therefore, is the solar life pouring into the world through the sign of Aries.

Continuing with Mr. Hall, "In the Persian execution of the Bull emblem, Mithras, the Sun-god, conquers the celestial Bull at the ancient vernal equinox." He said that Albert Pike describes the reverence which the Persians felt for this sign and the method of astrological symbolism in vogue among them. Thus, "In Zoroaster's Cave of initiation, the Sun and planets were represented, overhead, in gems and gold, as was also the zodiac. The Sun appeared emerging from the back of Taurus. In the constellation of the Bull are also to be found the 'Seven Sisters'—the sacred Pleiades—the star (Sun) group famous to Freemasonry of the ancient Egyptians as the Seven Stars at the end of the Sacred Ladder." We will discuss the Ladder symbol in another chapter. The goddess Isis of Egypt wears the horns of the Bull with the Sun orb between them as a headdress.

Stacey-Judd said that Bull worship was actually reverence to the constellation of Taurus in the astrological zodiac of the heavens. He also said that when seeking evidence concerning the connection between the Osiris cult and the Pyramid (of Gizeh), we must first turn to Plato. He mentions that in the caves of Spain and France we learn that the Bull was sacred to Cro-Magnon-Aurignacian man. The cult of the Bull changed to the Bison or Buffalo, and that was also a sacred object among the North American Indians.

Other people who revered the heavenly sign of Taurus the Bull, at the time of the vernal equinox, were the Hebres and the Philistines. At this time of the year we have the Christian Easter, Jewish Passover and May Day of various peoples, including the ancient Druids. All of these celebrate the quickening of new life, resurrection and rebirth of spring. The Druids celebrated December 25 also, which is the winter solstice feast day.

In returning to Stacey-Judd, we note that he describes and shows that there are strange and similar markings in design and architecture which contribute additional evidence in linking the early peoples of Europe and Asia Minor with the ancient civilizations of the Americas. He shows that there is an enormous abundance of evidence giving parallels in mythologies, ceremonies and feast days. The same practices in art and architecture of all the ancient civilizations and people of the world, all over the world, give strong emphasis upon a mother civilization, forerunning and giving heritage to those later to come into being. In Bali, the Bull is used in cremation ceremonies.

In Japanese symbolism, the Oxen or Bull personifies the stages of initiation in evolvement through incarnations toward the attainment of Buddhahood; believing that with enlightenment comes truth, no longer being deluded by false values, and becoming aware that all things are of the same essence. In Chinese symbolism, the Bull is led with a rein; first the hind quarters disappear, then more and more of the beast disappears until it is entirely gone and the person leading it is walking in the air.

In Egypt, Ra was the Sun god, but interchangeably Osiris would sometimes take that place. Mr. Hall said that when "Osiris was the Egyptian Sun God, and when he took upon himself the form of the Celestial Bull, he was declared to have been born in the body of

16

that beast. For this reason, when the astrologers erected the annual horoscope of Egypt, they chose the moment of this incarnation, ascertaining therefrom the pleasure of the God." Nandi and the children of Israel made offerings to a golden calf because they were released from Egypt in the age of the Bull. The Ishtar gate of Babylon is decorated with Bulls and Dragons (575 B.C.), which are celestial symbols.

I quote from Manly Hall: "In the Calivian rites, the initiates stood under specially prepared sacrificial gratings and were bathed in the blood of sacred Bulls. In the Eleusinian and Bacchic rites of Greece, the candidates took their vows in secrecy while standing upon the skins of newly sacrificed Bulls. In the Mithraic Mysteries of Persia, Mithras, the crucified Solar Savior-God, is depicted driving his sword into the heart of a Bull to remind the initiated philosopher that the vital force by which nature is maintained is mystically the blood of Taurus (the Bull)." (This is deep symbology.)

Mr. Hall continues, "The University of Oxford (England) derives its name because of the Mithraic and the Druidic figures of this animal (the Bull) discovered in the environs of the college. It is also assumed that the bleeding heart so conspicuous in Roman Catholicism was originally the heart of an Ox, but when in the procession of the Equinoxes the Lamb came to the angle (Aries, a sign of the zodiac), the heart of this creature was substituted for that of the Bull." (Taurus) (Now it becomes "washed in the blood of the Lamb.")

Manly Hall said, "In that age, during which the vernal equinox occurred in Aries (the Ram-Lamb), the Solar Divinity was represented as a golden haired youth, holding in one hand a Lamb, and in the other a shepherd's crook."

The four saints in the New Testament, representing the four cosmic points, solstices and equinoxes, are put into stained glass windows of churches. One is in a church in St. Louis, Missouri, and another window is in the Saint Louis Art Museum. There is one in a basilica in Florence, Italy, one in the Vatican and others elsewhere in the world. Christ is in the center of this display of sacred art, the cosmic myth of the summer and winter solstices, the autumnal and vernal equinoxes, which is the earth's journey around the Sun in a year. Christ has been represented as the Sun god just as Lord Gautama Buddha and other great personages.

The four evangelists also will be mentioned in the chapter of Numbers. These four evangelists are designated to have the following qualities:

I. Matthew—the Cherub (human), angel Ezekial—to know, clear vision, spiritual birth and the zodiacal sign of Aquarius.

II. Mark—the Lion—to dare, bravery—great world teachers—the Sun god and the zodiacal sign of Leo.

III. Luke—the Bull—to do—power, ascension and the zodiacal sign of Taurus.

IV. John—the Serpent (Eagle and Dove)—to keep silent, secrecy, death, and the zodiacal sign of Scorpio.

17

Robert Graves, author and famous Greek mythologist, said that the Greek island of Rhodes was the property of the moon goddess, Diana, until she was extended by the Hittite Sun-god, Tesup, who was worshipped as a Bull.

In Tantric Buddhism, there was an abuse of practice that eventually developed, but originally Yama rode the Bull with strict discipline, the Bull representing the energy of the world.

St. Thomas Aquinas was called the "dumb Ox" (Bull), but was actually a very brilliant person. In paintings he is sometimes shown with the Ox, the Sun on his breast, holding the chalice and books.

An important parallel among the different pantheons is the Egyptian Cow goddess of love and joy who is identified with the Greek goddess as Aphrodite and the Roman goddess Venus, according to Sir Wallis Budge, the famous Egyptologist.

Manly Hall said, and I quote, "Thousands of years before the birth of Christ, the Pagans adored this figure of life and beauty (the Lamb). On the day of the equinox they gathered in the squares before their temples crying out as with a single voice: 'All hail Lamb of God, which taketh away the sin of the world!' According to Zadkiel, 'In Aries, this was called Chrisna, from which, probably, the Greeks formed their Krios, a ram; from the Chaldee, Kresna is a throne, or seat of power; in allusion to the power of the Sun when in Aries, his exaltation.'"

According to Manly Hall, Jupiter Ammon is depicted with Rams' horns upon his forehead as with Isis of Egypt. The Moses of Michelangelo is similarly adorned. Jupiter Pan, or lord of the world (the symbol of the generating power of the Sun), was represented as a Goat-man. The astrological sign of Capricorn in the zodiac is depicted as a Goat, and its ruling planet is Saturn, bringing about life's lessons and learning through evolutionary trials and tests.

We return to Manly Hall, who said that "In Greek mysticism, the Golden Fleece is directly related to the ritual of Aries (Ram-Lamb). This fleece is the wool of the wise; the same wool which was pulled over the eyes of the foolish."

"After passing 2,160 years in the sign of the Ram (Lamb) the heavenly rotations caused the vernal equinox to take place in Pisces and during that period the 'Light of the World' appeared as the 'Fisher of Men.' The world has just passed through the Piscean cycle, which by the very nature of the sign has been an age of travail, for Pisces (the Fish) is the last zodiacal sign and is the sidereal instrument of retribution." Cosmic mythology is found in astrology.

Aquarius is an air sign, and we are presently in the transition period between Pisces and Aquarius. Some key words of this sign, the period to come, are "invention," "mysticism," "electric," "heavenly water," (or the "living waters" as spoken of previously), and this sign, well aspected, can bring with it brotherhood and advancement.

OTHER ANIMALS

As the Ram became the symbol of the leader of the flock of heaven, after Taurus the Bull, it was thus recognized in Egypt as well as in other nations of antiquity. This was the symbol of Moses, and when Michelangelo sculptured him with horns (a statue in San Pietro in Vincali, Rome), it was with deliberate intent and not a mistake.

In American Indian symbology, we find ceremonial paintings with a horned figure in conjunction with a Serpent and the Sun, as with deities in Egypt; Osiris with the Ureas (Serpent) also has Bull horns and Sun headdress.

There is a ferocious looking Oriental deity whirling out of the clouds who is also wearing horns. This figure demonstrates one of the forces of nature. He holds the double dorje in his hand, which is also in the hand of a pre-Columbian clay figure.

The Egyptian Jackal-headed deity has the same connotation as the fox featured in early European, Scandinavian and Slavic fairy tales! He is the guide and protector of the neophyte through tests and travail toward peace, balance and happiness.

To the Deer has been assigned the same meaning as the Unicorn, symbolic of the soul, elusive, timid and residing in the forest. In Celtic mythology the advanced entity is shown wearing Deer antlers (from *Celtic Mythology* by MacCana). The symbol of the Deer is used in the mythology of Egypt, the Scythians, India, the Orient, Greek, American Indian, and Roman. It is the goddess Artemis (Greek) or Diana (Roman) who is accompanied by a Deer. She is the goddess of the Moon and the hunt. This representation is to typify the pure virgin spirit that hunts for wisdom and knowledge. The great teacher of the Orient, Lord Gautama Buddha, is often pictured as a Deer.

Katherine Ball, in her *Decorative Motives of Oriental Art,* relates that the legends of the Hare or Rabbit are found in allegorical tales (and in zodiacs of different countries) coming from India, China, Japan, Mexico, the ancient Aztecs, South Africa, Egypt, the Hottentot tribes, and in England and Germany. She gives allegories in which the Hare is both fortunate and unfortunate in the interpretations. The Hare is associated with the Moon, and, in the zodiac, it is connected to the fourth house which is under the sign of Cancer, ruled by the Moon. It is its leaping about in different directions, suddenly, that gives a resemblance to the sudden fluctuating moods of the diverse phases of the Moon, being quickly changeable in character as the Moon changes.

The Mirror in Japan in Shintoism and in Hinduism and other cultures is sacred because it stands for the Moon reflecting the solar energy as well as the soul reflecting the solar energy. The solar plexus is also ruled by the Moon. The Aztecs had an obsidian Mirror for sacred ceremonies and conjuring spirits.

Ball said that the Egyptians, like the Chinese, were also attracted by the starting eyes of the Hare, which were regarded as significant of the opening, or the beginning of events and periodicity, particularly with reference to pubescence. It is associated with the life-opening period and the beginning of another year. Hence the European custom of celebrating earth with the Rabbit and the Egg.

Ball also expressed that it is interesting to note that the ancient Aztecs likewise held the Hare in high esteem. It was one of the four chief signs symbolizing the four elements, known as "Tochtli," the Hare, and dedicated to "Tevacoyohua," the god of earth. The other signs were "Calli," the house, dedicated to "Xintencli," god of fire; "Tecptl," the flint, dedicated to "Quetzalcoatl," the god of air, and "Actal," the cane, dedicated to "Laloc," the god of water. The Maya used the symbol, the Feathered Serpent, Quetzalcoatl, of air and water.

The Moon has many kinds of influences, but in the physical alone it affects the tides, a powerful force of cosmic energy pulling on the oceans, also regulating the fluids of the body, the cycles of women, the weather, and planting.

The Rabbit frequently has been painted in Japanese Sumi style of watercolor, in mythological artwork, and it figures prominently in Japanese fairy tales and allegories. The Rabbit is also on European tapestries; it is the Rabbit (Easter Bunny) which brings Eggs (Auric) to children in rainbow colors at the spring season (vernal equinox) when the Bull of Taurus gores open the Cosmic Egg for the new life or rebirth. The constellation of the Hare (Lepus) is in the Southern Hemisphere of the heavens in relation to our planet.

The Elephant is revered by the Hindu, Maya, Chinese, and Japanese. The Elephant god, Ganesha, is the center of the solar system, the Sun; this is the sign of royalty, generosity and intelligence.

It was the Elephant on a silver cloud who appeared to the mother of Buddha, who was called Maya. He told her she had conceived immaculately from the Holy Spirit and that she would give birth to a great world teacher. He was born Prince Sidhartha before finally becoming the Buddha.

In a quarterly journal *(The Horizon)* published by Manly P. Hall, Winter 1945, was an article entitled "The Mystery of the Disappearing Elephants." He describes a monolith or stele (B) of high-relief carving on stone found in the old Maya city of Copan. On each side of the elaborate headdress of an heroic figure, a god, was the beautifully carved forepart of elephants. Mr. Hall quotes from J. Leslie Mitchell's interesting book, *The Conquest of the Mayas*: "They are unmistakably [East] Indian surmounted by mahouts complete with turbans and goads; they are beasts of a sculptor who had never seen them in the dun flesh, might record from legend."

Since there are no elephants in America except those which have been imported for zoos and circuses, Mr. Hall said that a violent argument has raged in high places for many years. The stone sculpture has been very upsetting to Mayaologists and other gentry of the learned because they cannot understand how an East Indian Elephant happens to be on a Maya work of sacred art in Central America. The mastodon and mammoth which roamed the Americas are different from the East Indian pachyderm and had been extinct for thousands of years before the appearance of the builders of the mysterious Maya civilization. He asked how the classical American Indians found models for their artistry of the East Indian Elephant. He thought that it also seemed unlikely that turbaned mahouts rode mastodons, and added—

"But then science is flexible"! He noted that the Elephant heads looked exactly like what they were intended to represent, but another scientific group suggested that they were intended to be macaws, tapirs or alligators.

As he looked at the curling trunks, he was delighted with the thought that the Mayas might have conceived of alligators with their tails at the wrong end! But he recognized that the most intriguing thought was that the Elephant heads are *really Elephant heads*.

Again Mr. Hall quotes Mr. Mitchell, whose word is given weight by the fact that his book has a foreword by Professor G. Elliot Smith, M.A., M.D., D.S.C., etc.: "They are— or rather, they *were*. The elephant decoration on stele (B) was badly mutilated by 'bandits.' " Mitchell was suspicious, and Mr. Hall believed that there may be some truth lurking behind the substance of Mitchell's suspicions, saying that when things cannot be explained, it is simpler, although less scientific, to destroy the evidence rather than hazard the dignity of that state of fragmentary information which we like to call fact.

Many know of the wisdom and memory and almost human temperament of the Elephant; that they have nurses, raise their trunks and kiss in courtship, have leaders, burial grounds, and can be trained. In the Autumn 1960 issue of the *PRS Journal,* Manly Hall explains that in India, the Elephant is closely associated with Ganesha, the Elephant head deity ruling over wisdom, good fortune and shrewd merchandising. In Burma, the Elephant is regarded as a Buddhist symbol, and some not of the most approved color are used as beasts of burden. Once they are given a task and they understand what they are supposed to do, they need very little supervision. Mr. Hall watched Burmese Elephants stack teakwood logs on a pile, step back and carefully survey their work, and then with their trunks arrange the pile so that no log was in the slightest way out of alignment.

He writes that Pliny regards the Elephant as the only animal practicing religion with the exception of the gorilla. At certain seasons the Elephant went to available water supplies and bathed itself. On the night of the full moon, herds formed in what appeared to be a congregation and, raising their trunks to the moon in unison, swayed their bodies and trumpeted loudly. They have come to be regarded as moon worshippers.

The Elephant is a brave yet timid animal, kindly and with a sense of humor. The animal, Mr. Hall recounts, is very conscious of dignity and honor, and he says there are accounts that in state processionals an Elephant who is accustomed to walking in the third place will lie down and sob like a baby if he is demoted to fourth or fifth position. He makes no objection, however, to advancement.

Further, Mr. Hall said there are cases known in which Elephants pursued by ivory hunters showed almost superhuman wisdom. They would hide temporarily and break off their own tusks to save their lives.

It is no wonder then that the Elephant has been greatly revered and used as a symbol representing the highest of all qualities.

Great world heroes such as Ulysses, Buddha, Hercules (Herakles Greek counterpart),

Krishna, and others have at times been shown wearing a Lion or Leopard skin, which symbolically indicated the power which they had gained from having become developed within themselves. Hercules, for example, strangled the Nemian Lion (Greece, 525 B.C.), powerful but harmless. The Lion is the symbol of strength, and Hercules is sometimes shown with his head in the mouth of a Lion. Jesus has often been shown with Lions as well as being a Lion.

Allegories were woven for a deep and wonderful purpose; they were not reporting as literal realities—strange exploits of the gods of antiquity who were put into stories of deliberate concealments.

In the New Testament, the Revelations of St. John, the Lion is said to be the root of David, David the builder and the tribe of Judah.

Even today, those in the British Fife and Drum Corps in Gibraltar have uniforms that consist in part of small Leopard capes. The royal family has been designated power to rule by the people, and the music they play is the music of the royal family. Some Scottish pipe regiments also have similar Leopard uniforms.

Under the feline species are Lions, Tigers, Leopards, Jaguars, Panthers, Cheetahs, and Cats, all used in ancient symbolism. All ancient civilizations used this animal as the symbol of power, energy, essence, great world teachers, and the Sun.

In the priesthood of the ancient Maya civilization of Central America, they are shown wearing Leopard and Jaguar skins. The Jaguar was also a symbol in Peru. There are Lion Gates at Mycenae, Lion Gates of the Hittite civilization, and the Lion of Hercules in Rome (Herakles of Greece). Leopard skins were worn by leaders of African tribes. The Cat in Egypt was originally revered as a symbol personifying the Universe because of its attributes as curling in a circle, seeing in the dark, with sparks of light (electricity) coming from its fur. To the Cheetah in Egypt is assigned leadership and power.

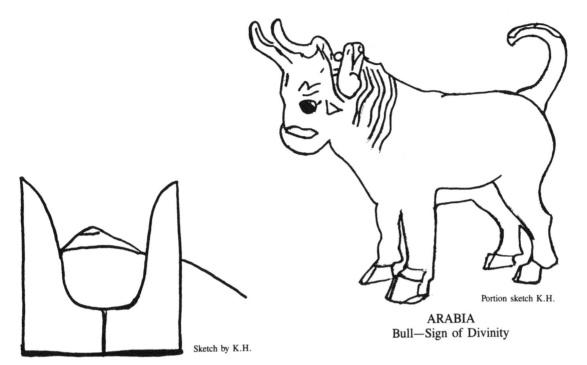

Portion sketch K.H.

ARABIA
Bull—Sign of Divinity

Portion sketch K.H.

American Indian
Buffalo Horns

Sketch by K.H.

Giant "Horns of Consecration." Mount
Jouctas is visible between the horns.
Palace, Knossos, Crete

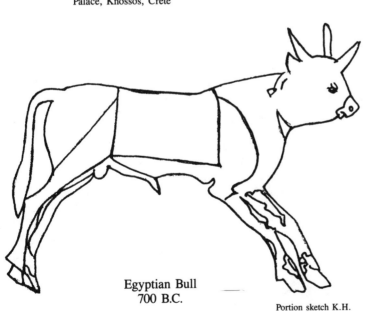

Egyptian Bull
700 B.C.

Portion sketch K.H.

23

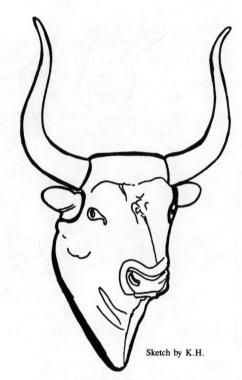

Sketch by K.H.

Sacred Bull—Knossos—Greece
Crete, Small Palace

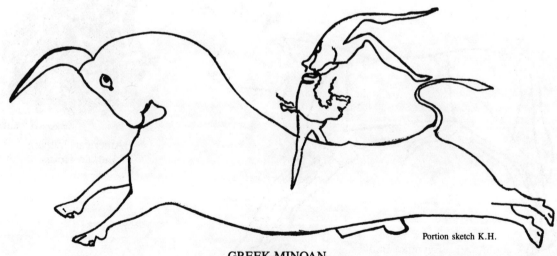

Portion sketch K.H.

GREEK-MINOAN
Bull leaping. About 1500 B.C.
Fresco—Palace of Minos—Knossos, Crete

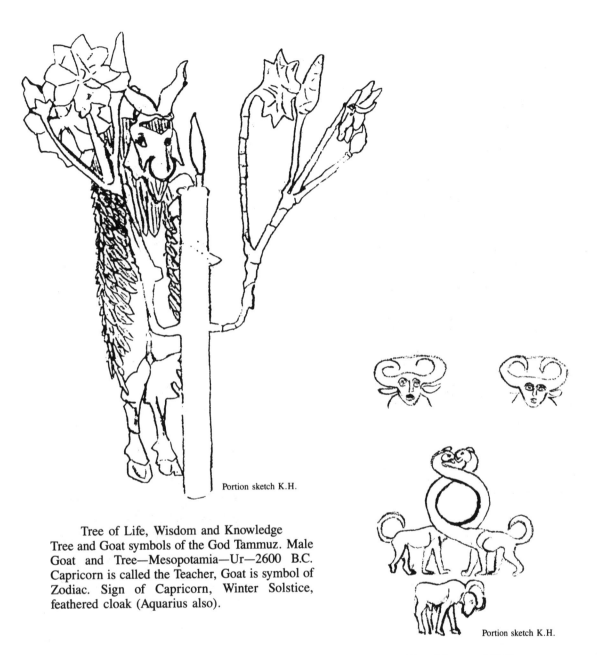

Portion sketch K.H.

Tree of Life, Wisdom and Knowledge
Tree and Goat symbols of the God Tammuz. Male
Goat and Tree—Mesopotamia—Ur—2600 B.C.
Capricorn is called the Teacher, Goat is symbol of
Zodiac. Sign of Capricorn, Winter Solstice,
feathered cloak (Aquarius also).

Portion sketch K.H.

Two Lions and Bull
Early Egyptian dynasty. Heads with Bull horns
on ears. Originally Mesopotamian.

25

EGYPTIAN
Hathor—Cow Goddess (Taurus), Sun and
Horned Headdress.

Portion sketch K.H.

EGYPTIAN BIRD
Falcon (the God Horus) on head of a Priest
King. Thrones and heads of rulers often
had the lion motif.

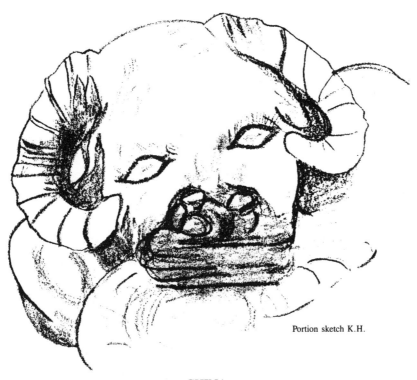

Portion sketch K.H.

CHINA
Head of Bull—Jade. The complete carving of the Bull is in a reclining position.
DeYoung Museum, Avery Brundage Collection

Prehistoric Bull.
Museum Fiorentino di Prehistoria, Florence, Italy

27

Partial sketch K.H.

Buffalo headdress of American Indian.
Outline sketch K.H.

Chief Sitting Bull (Buffalo) was actually
a Medicine Man and a great person.
Single feather.
Sketched from picture in National Archives.

K.H.

Sun Design. Partial sketch of
sand painting for healing by
Southwest American Indians.
Sketched from photo by Ray Manley.

Sketch by K.H.

Egyptian Stag and Gazelle headbands for
princesses. Similar to Rosette bands of Greek
and Etruscan.
(In Metropolitan Museum of Art)

Bull, Northern Greece, Tomb of Alexander.
Also found there is gold wreath with oak
leaves. Symbol of the Druids.

28

Pope Gregory listening to the inspiration of the Holy Ghost through the Dove.

CAMBODIA
Bull
Photo by Clarke Johnston

Portion sketch
K.H.

The White Bull (Zeus)—Greek allegory. The Rape of Europa—from whence the continent of Europe got its name.

Titian

29

Partial rough
sketch by K.H.

The Four Evangelists, Matthew, Mark, Luke and John, with their animal
symbols, the Bull, Eagle, Lion, and Cherubim. The two solstices and two
equinoxes.

Basilica of St. Croce, Italy

30

EGYPT
Plaque of three metals designed after throne panel of
Tutankhamun. Lion paw legs on throne chair. Decor
of disks, cobras and feathered headdresses. The Sun,
Aton, has rays ending in human hands.
Collection of Mr. and Mrs. John Trent

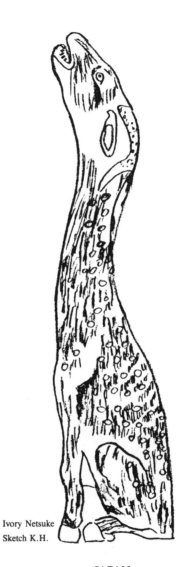

Ivory Netsuke
Sketch K.H.

JAPAN
Stag—The Soul
Metropolitan Museum of Art

Lioness by Marianne
Photo by Harry W. Henry

Sketch by K.H.

Enormous baptismal font for the dead in the Mormon Salt Lake City Temple resting on the backs of twelve oxen symbolizing the tribes of Israel. (This is also the zodiacal sign of Taurus.)

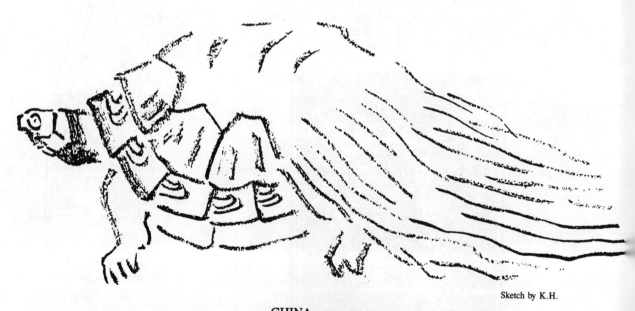

Sketch by K.H.

CHINA
Turtle of the World
Philosophical Research Society

Animal Symbolism. Heavenly Constellations and
Zodiac Animals.

Printed in Italy.

Partial outline sketch
K.H.

JAPAN
Elephant and the Blind Men
Metropolitan Museum of Art

Partial outline sketch
K.H.

JAPAN
The Fox and sacred Sword. Swords and spears
are in many mythologies which sever the lower
emotions (seed atom in liver area) from the
spiritual qualities. The Fox is also in Russian
and Scandinavian mythologies.

Metropolitan Museum of Art

33

Partial sketch
K.H.

Mosaic of Lions at the feet of Daniel
Church of Hosios Lukas—Greece

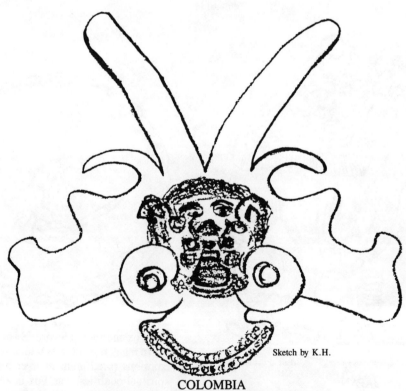

Sketch by K.H.

COLOMBIA
Outline of gold breastplate Lion with open mouth.
Gift of Morton D. May, St. Louis Art Museum

34

Sketch by K.H.

MAYA
Hieroglyphic symbol of eclipse of the
Sun. Similar to Japanese Dragon
swallowing moon.

Sketch by K.H.

Ram—horned—plumed head-
dress. Crocodile deity of
Egypt.

Sketch—part of pendant from Peru.
Bird-like deity with domed headdress.

Field Museum of Natural History—Chicago

Sketch by K.H.

EGYPT
Stele of the Serpent King with
Hawk.
Louvre Museum

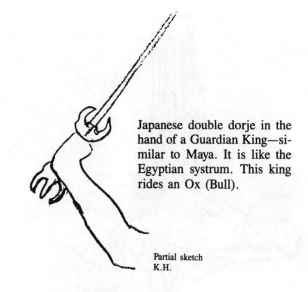

Japanese double dorje in the hand of a Guardian King—similar to Maya. It is like the Egyptian systrum. This king rides an Ox (Bull).

Partial sketch
K.H.

Partial sketch
K.H.

Japanese head of scepter. Sacred object used in many civilizations.

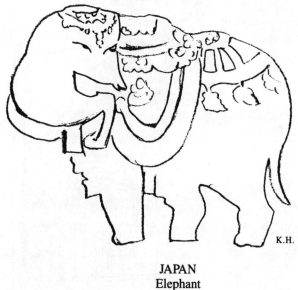

K.H.

JAPAN
Elephant

There is a Maya bas-relief sculpturing on stone showing the elephant (which we know today) which did not exist on this continent at that time, only the mastedon and mammoth, which were roaming the land 15,000 to 20,000 years ago.

Sketch by K.H.

MAYA
Masked ceremony of Elephant and Leopard, symbols of wisdom and power.

36

Tutankhamun, the King, is displayed here in the guise of the advanced Soul or Deity, as both male and female, in gold, with headdress of the Priest, the sacred implements, shepherd's crook, and flail and standing upon a Feline (black Leopard) or Panther, of power. The same power given to the Jaguar, Tiger, Lion, and Cat; symbolizing the Sun, Universe, and Teachers of Divine rank.

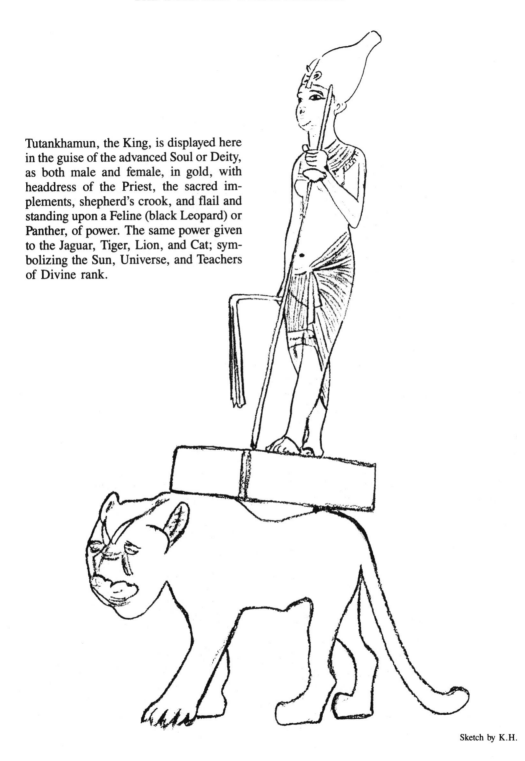

Sketch by K.H.

Partial outline sketch
K.H.

Jade boulder carving showing sacred Buddhist elements in symbolism. The power of the Lion is leashed and under control. The stairs are the tests the soul must pass for higher attainment in evolvement. The Bodhisattva meditating in the cave is wisdom; there are caves in many ancient philosophies and religions. The Bodhisattva of benevolence is riding the Elephant of wisdom and royalty, holding the magical Sceptre of power and is protected by the sacred Umbrella. There is the Tree of Life and Wisdom and the Mountain (the head) wherein Wisdom resides. The three-leveled Pagoda is the Golden Pagoda of the Heart wherein the Spirit of God resides.

Avery Brundage Collection, DeYoung Memorial Museum

There is another carving in the Avery Brundage Collection of the DeYoung Museum of Lapis Lazuli from China showing a Mountain, a Crane (Bird—Soul), Pine Trees (Tree of Everlasting Life and Wisdom), and the Deer (the Soul). In the Orient, Jade is the symbol of Purity.

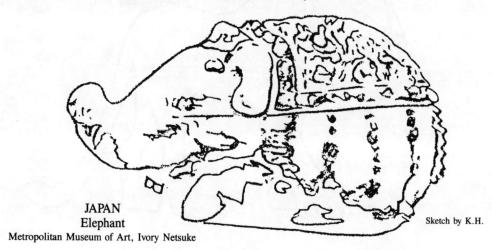

JAPAN
Elephant
Metropolitan Museum of Art, Ivory Netsuke

Sketch by K.H.

38

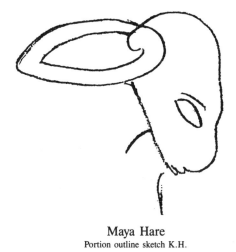

Maya Hare
Portion outline sketch K.H.

JAPAN
The Hare. Associated with the Moon.
Metropolitan Museum of Art, Ivory Netsuke

EGYPT
SACRED SYMBOLIC ANIMALS AND PLANT LIFE

The Bee. One of the symbols of Egypt. In antiquity the Bee symbolized the wise men gathering wisdom from experiences as the Bee gathers pollen from flower to flower.

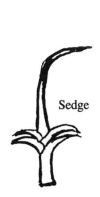

Falcon

Vulture

Cobra

Sedge

Portion Sketches by K.H.

39

From the *Philosophical Research Society Bulletin,* December, 1968, by Manly P. Hall:

Like all such psychical images, ordinary problems in no way damage the folk lore. If there is no fireplace, Santa Claus is not thwarted. And in this day of rapid transit, the problem of going around the world in a single night, in a sleigh drawn by reindeer, causes no anxiety. Like the Bodhisattvas, Santa Claus can be anywhere and everywhere and always. Like them he can be infinitely multiplied until he is a veritable legion. Yet actually there are no facsimilies and no impostures if the spirit is right. The Santa Claus ringing the bell on the street by the Salvation Army kettle, the Santa Claus bringing food baskets to the poor, the Santa Claus who listens to the requests of small children in a toy shop, are all real, genuine and valid. Like the venerable Pu, Santa Claus abides in the young of heart, the generous of soul and the kindly of mind.

Another East-West parallel is most intriguing. Santa Claus is supposed to live at the North Pole, a bleak and inhospitable region, where it is dark for nearly half of the year. This certainly must be another instance of Hoben. In ancient India the great polar mountain of the earth was Meru or Sumuro, the axis of the world. On the sides of this mountain dwelt the Hindu Immortals and in the course of time the Buddhist contemplation images were given the same abode. From this mountain were sent streams of life that made all the world fertile. Here were the treasure palaces from which streamed forth blessings upon all living creatures. What more fitting place could be found for the workshop of Santa Claus, for are we not also children, dependent upon the generosity of a divine plan for our very existence?

Yet another analogy seems pertinent. In these speedy days, Santa Claus still depends upon a team of reindeer to bring his heavily laden sleigh across the sky and into the lives of believing children. The deer has long been a Christian symbol to signify by its gentleness the gracious patience suitable to the devout believer. The deer is also one of the earliest and most important symbols of Buddhism. It was in the Deer Park at Sarnath, near Benares, that Gautama Buddha preached his first sermon. Here for the first time he "turned the wheel of the Law," revealing to five Monks the doctrines of reincarnation and karma. Everywhere in Eastern painting and sculpturing, the deer attends Buddha, usually kneeling near the base of the Lotus upon which the Great Teacher is seated. In some cases the deer is actually substituted for Buddha. A recent example of this process is a postage stamp of Thailand, in which the deer takes the place of the Buddha image.

ANCIENT
GREEK
COINS

Alexander the Great with Ram's horn. This was the symbol of the Egyptian god Ammon. Astrological symbol of Aries, the Ram or Lamb.

Persephone and Dolphins. Fish is the astrological symbol of Pisces.

Stylized Lion's head. Astrological symbol of Leo.

Herakles (Hercules) wrestling with and conquering the Nemean Lion. Astrological symbol of Leo, representing the attainment of leadership and power, here, and also the Teacher.

Reverse of Persephone coin. Chariot drawn by four Horses. The chariot driver is being crowned by Nike (Victory). Each of the four horses are symbols in Egyptian (Gnostic) teaching and the Bible as well as in Greek philosophy.

Bull symbol kicking stones. Astrological symbol of Taurus.

Rough sketches by K.H.

For more information on these, refer to *These Were the Greeks* by H.D. Amos and A.G.P. Lang.

Elephant
of
India

Sketch by K.H.

Sketch by K.H.

Woolly Mammoth
Northern Eurasia and North America. Extinct
thousands of years prior to the Maya civilization.

Sketch by K.H.

American Mastodon
Extinct thousands of years prior to the Maya
civilization.

42

MYTHOLOGICAL CREATURES AND
THE SERPENT, SNAKE AND DRAGON

MYTHOLOGICAL CREATURES

There is a variety of composites of unreal creatures giving evidence of great truths, not immediately obvious. The symbols have wonderful meanings behind them. These are not real animals. Fables and fairy tales meant only for minds which could discriminate between the real and unreal were not intended for children.

There are griffins, sphinxes, winged creatures of all kinds, unicorns, fish-goats, serpents, dragons, harpies, sirens, cyclops, mermaids, mermen, centaurs, satyrs, a minotaur, a three-headed dog, a three-footed toad, and more.

In Egypt, there are the jackel-headed and bird-headed deities, plus the human Cow goddess already mentioned in the complicated allegorical pantheon. In Egypt, Babylonia, Persia, India, and other ancient cultures, we find amongst the ruins today the sphinxes and griffins which are symbolized with animal, human and spiritual qualities combined. There are Sphinx sculptures throughout civilizations of antiquity being composites also of winged animals, Lions, Serpents and human beings.

From Greece is the three-headed dog of Hades and the Minotaur, half-man, half-bull who dwelt in the labyrinth at Knossos, son of a Bull and Pasiphae.

In China and Japan are the "Lion Dogs" of Fu who guard the temple and the temple of the soul (being neither Lion nor Dog). These represent the two major forces of the Universe, the positive and the negative. The male Lion-dog often has his paw on a sphere, the energy of powerful force which the ball signifies, while the female Lioness-dog fondles her cub, giving expression to the gentler elements of nature. This is a symbolic expression of "the pairs of opposites," which are many; a few examples are hot and cold, sweet and sour, and "good" and "evil" (which are interchangeable), male and female, etc. In China, it is the Yin and the Yang.

In antiquity, the Bee was the symbol of the wise man or advanced soul who went from experience to experience gathering wisdom as the Bee gathers pollen from flower to flower. King Solomon in the Holy Bible bowed his head in reverence to the Bee and commented that there was nothing too great or too small that had nothing to give. There is also an insect in the Maya legends, and there is the Spider Woman of the Hopi Amerindian.

The All-Seeing Eye is mentioned in the Homeric legend where Odysseus (Ulysses) encounters the Cyclops Polyphemus (one-eyed giant). It is also on an ornament of Tutukhamon, being a symbol of the Sun and representing the ductless gland which is called the pituitary body.

The famed mythological Unicorn of both China and European Renaissance is said to portray the advanced human soul, shy and hidden in the forest, of a mind one-pointedness, the horn protruding from the pituitary body wherein lies the All-Seeing Eye. Oftentimes it is shown with a maiden (the human soul).

The All-Seeing Eye is sometimes displayed in the palm of the hand of an advanced Christian soul, in the blessing posture and holding a Cross.

There is an amazing picture of Jesus with the All-Seeing Eye in the Uffici Gallery in Florence, Italy. In India, there is a temple with All-Seeing Eyes painted all around it. The dollar bill in the United States has a picture of the pyramid of Gizeh with the All-Seeing Eye on the capstone. There is also the Eye of Horus, an Egyptian deity.

Dr. C. G. Jung on the Unicorn:

A. The Unicorn in alchemy of the European Middle Ages.
B. The Unicorn in ecclesiastical allegory of European Middle Ages.
C. The Unicorn in Gnosticism (ancient Egypt).
D. The one-horned Scarabarus (Egyptian and Greek).
E. The Unicorn in the Vedas (Hinduism, the Fish of Manu was unicorned; Manu means "man," and the Fish is an incarnation of Vishnu.).
F. The Unicorn in Persia.
G. The Unicorn in Jewish tradition.
H. The Unicorn in China.
I. The Unicorn cup (eucharistic chalice), "Cup of Salvation" and vessel used in divination. The lunar Unicorn is shown with the maiden and moon crescent and the celestial horn of the Moon.

In Greek mythology, the winged Horse, Pegasus, carries the advanced soul, Bellerophon, through the air to the heights of a Mountain where the Horse smotes the earth with his hoof and from whence gushes a fountain of water from a spring. This procedure occurred to Moses on the Mountain, as the living waters poured from a rock. Pegasus kills the Chimera, the Lion with the Serpent's tail, and is shown with Cerebus, the three-headed Dog. Pegasus is also with Athena and Persephone in different allegories.

In the Revelations of St. John in the New Testament, the Four Horsemen of the Apocalypse and their colors are very meaningful.

The Phoenix Bird of the Oriental and Egyptian had the nest of fire and the five sacred colors in its plumage. It rises from the dross and ashes, purified by the flames, into a new birth; it is the symbol of the advanced soul, the initiate and adept. It is the Golden Firebird of the Slavic peoples and also is found in the mythology of Arabia.

CAT
Alice in Wonderland by Ollie Arabsky Dwiggins (drawing).

RABBIT
Alice in Wonderland by Ollie Arabsky Dwiggins (drawing).

46

THE SERPENT, SNAKE AND DRAGON

The famous Serpent is one of the most interesting symbolical and mythological objects in the teaching of philosophy and religion of many ancient civilizations. Coiled upon the foreheads of Egyptian priest-kings and priestess-queens is the Serpentine uraeus, symbol of achievement. The real animal as well as mythological is used for this vital symbol.

In the Gnostic group of Egypt, from which much of Christianity has descended, there is the Cock symbol with Serpent legs driving four horses. The Cock is also a symbol in the Christian Bible.

There are dragons of the Celts in *The Book of Kells* and a double Serpent on the Christian chalice, the symbol of St. John, as told by Manly Hall and also George Ferguson in *Signs and Symbols in Christian Art.*

In Egypt, there is a decor of cobras alternating with feathers, and the single feather is worn by goddesses. Not only was this done in Egypt, but the single feather was worn by the American Indian. This was to indicate the union of the pineal gland and the pituitary body in the brain, resulting in the manifestation of great power which also came in juxtaposition from the disciples of universal law. The practice of shaved heads by monks in the Middle Ages was for the same reason as the wearing of the single feather by the Amerindian. The symbol of the Pine cone has the same meaning in American Indian and Roman symbology.

The Seven-headed Serpent as the creator, the maker, is found among the ancient Maya, Hindu and Greek civilizations (the Seven-headed Serpent of Hercules). The Serpent symbol is also found in Burma, Babylonia and among the North, Central and South American Indians. It is the symbol of the Seven original planets of the Solar System which will be elaborated upon further in the book.

Max Müller wrote that one should never judge any of the ancient religions from appearances. He said that faith, sacrifice and love in the heart is true religion, not the dogmas, doctrines and creeds that man has made or what is recorded as so-called history which is really of unhistorical essence. Madame Blavatsky said there is no religion higher than truth.

The mythology of Dragons, Serpents, Snakes, and Crocodiles was never intended for the reading or the understanding of children, to amuse them, such as "The Dragon's Teeth" and many more. These are allegories to teach deep meanings, as with the other fairy tales mentioned.

The plumed Crocodile of Egypt and the plumed Feathered Serpent (Quetzalcoatl-Kukulcan) of the pre-Columbian Maya are symbolic expressions of the actual attainment of the lower self having been conquered—a gaining of control of the self, instead of being devoured. It is similar and compared to the Chinese in taming the Dragon, which then results in bringing great power and goodness. This is the Dragon that follows the priest-ruler as would a pet dog.

A pendant from the tomb of Tutankhamon has on it a Serpent goddess with a human head suckling Tutankhamon. The Minoan civilization (Greek island of Crete) had a Snake mother-goddess.

The Serpent in a vertical position on tombstones, in the original sense in antiquity, represented advanced souls, and they were called Snakes because of the Kundalini (Hindu term) that entwined up the spine. This is shown as a double Serpent of the Caduceus or Escalapian staff (used today by the medical profession). They were the snakes who disappeared into a hole in the heavens, as explained by Helena Petrovna Blavatsky in *The Secret Doctrine* and *Isis Unveiled* when speaking of initiates and adepts.

In lieu of the Cobra of Egypt and the Cobra of India, Madame Blavatsky said that advanced souls raised the Kundalini to the brain, the Serpentine qualities touching off the Seven chakras of the spine. In the Hindu belief as well as beliefs in other civilizations who had the same symbol, the red essence, called the coiled Serpent of Kundalini, is at the base of the spine. When raised, it reaches the brain in blue and gold essence, as two Serpents emerge from the coiled Kundalini and ascend the spine, forming the Caduceus or Escalapian staff. Topped with globe, wings and a rosy hue, the symbol of the Rose Croix is formed.

Bika Reed, Manly Hall and many other authors show a Serpent biting its tail, a symbol of the Universe of ancient Egypt and Persia.

The Serpent has slithered its way through civilizations, philosophies and religions and taken wings across oceans to various continents. This symbol stands for the *lower nature of man,* his passions and greeds; it stands also for his *higher nature* as well as for *creation.* It is the Dragon, writhing and twisting through the heavens as solar systems and galaxies. It is their birth, existence, their death (the black hole or "coal sack"), and their rebirth, according to the ancients, Madame Blavatsky and other authors of note.

In the Orient, the Dragon is a symbol that is predominantly used and prominently placed in and around temples. In the Christian Bible, there is St. George and the Dragon, the Seven-headed Dragon, the Serpent with the human head coiling around the Tree (fruit tree) in the Garden of Eden, St. Margaret and the Serpent, St. Charles of Toulouse who is standing on a basilisk reptilian creature (Saint Louis Art Museum), and the Virgin who not only stands on the Moon and crescent Venus, but in another instance on a Serpent. In Greece, we have the Gorgon's head called Medusa (whose hair is twisting Snakes), who is finally beheaded by Perseus with the sword of truth and the shield of virtue as with St. George. Both Mithras, the Persian Savior, and Serapis, the Egyptian god of the earth, were symbolized by Serpents and often shown with Serpents coiled about their bodies. There is a Serapis of Egypt and a Serapis of Greece. Both the Egyptian and Greek Hermes are also shown with a foot on a reptilian creature. In India, the nine-headed Cobra moves in space with the god Vishnu on his back. The Hopi, American Indian, today still demonstrate the ceremonial Snake dance, and there is the great Serpent Mound built by Amerindians in Ohio. The Indians of Central America worshipped their Savior, "Quetzalcoatl" (Maya) or "Kukulcan" (Aztec), the feathered Serpent. In allegories shown on European tapestries and in their paintings, when Dragons are being slain, there is often a lady in the picture, as with the Unicorn. The damsel in distress is the soul which is to be rescued by coming into control with universal law, to work with it and for it.

In the *History of Britain* by Sir George Clarke (and edited with additional material by Dr. J. N. Westwood), Oxford University Press, there is shown a mosaic floor in the main room of a Roman villa recently excavated at Lullingstone in Kent. They describe the villa as having been built 100 A.D., but the floor having been laid in a new room about 350 A.D. It pictures Bellerophon seated on his winged horse, Pegasus, slaying the monster, Chimera, which is said to be the Roman equivalent of St. George and the Dragon.

As with all symbols, myths and allegories, being so numerous, it would be impossible to list them all; a book of them would be the size of a house, so we enumerate only some of them even though we would like to go on and on with these fascinating discoveries.

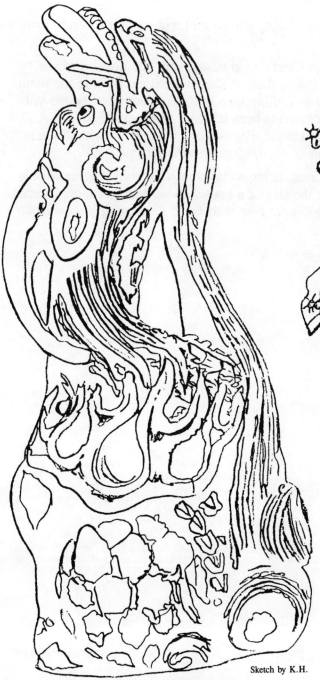

Portion sketch outline
K.H.

The Flying Horse of the Zodiac
The symbol of inspiration and philosophy—
Sagittarius.

Sketch by K.H.

Mythological Creature Kirin
Japanese version of Unicorn, symbol of the soul-evolve-
ment. Parts of Horse, Lion, Deer and Dragon.
Metropolitan Museum of Art

50

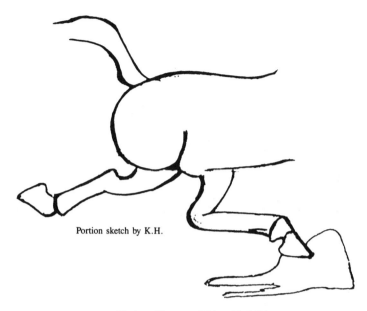

Portion sketch by K.H.

Flying Horse—China Exhibit
Similar to Greek Pegasus. Representing advanced soul.
Portion outline from touring exhibit. William Rockhill Nelson Museum.

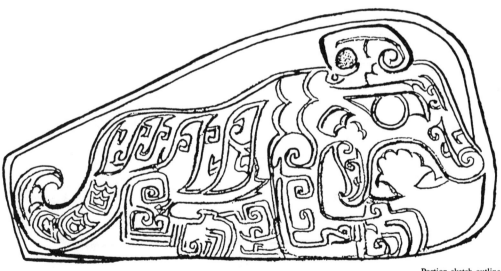

Portion sketch outline
K.H.

Tiger—China
Similar to ancient Maya Feline symbol.

Portion sketch, K.H.

Tiny ceremonial Bell. Maya-Toltec artifacts found in sacred wall at Chichén Itzá.

From photographs by
Phillip Harrington.

Sketch by K.H.

MAYA

Perhaps this is Spider Woman who lived in a cave and gave prophecy to advanced souls as did the Greek Delphic Oracles. The Sun Goddess of Japan lived in a cave, in the allegory; after emerging, she gave light to the world.

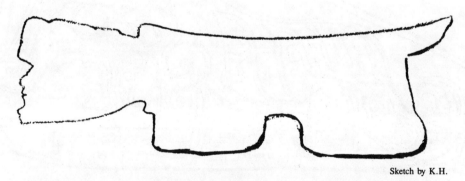

Sketch by K.H.

A ceremonial stool with the head of Kukulcan (Quetzalcoatl) emerging from a serpent body. He is the Feathered Serpent Deity of living waters.

52

MYTHOLOGICAL BIRDS

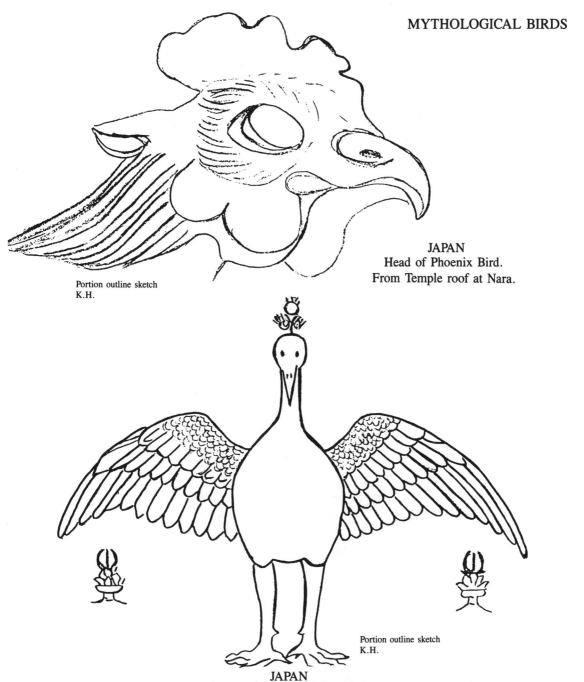

JAPAN
Head of Phoenix Bird.
From Temple roof at Nara.

Portion outline sketch
K.H.

Portion outline sketch
K.H.

JAPAN
The Peacock King, a deity, rides in Lotus position on Lotus atop the Peacock with tail in full spread as Throne. The Peacock is chosen as a symbol because of the eyes in the tail feathers. It is like the Phoenix Bird (mythological) as symbolic of the advanced soul or deity.

53

Sketch by K.H.

The Golden Bird or Bird of Fire
Three stories by Wilhelm and Jacob Grimm from *Journeys Through Bookland* are from an ancient fairy tale of Slavic origin, "Ohnivak." There are similar tales from the Orient, China. "The Phoenix" which is much more ancient and from the Sufi, "The Language of the Birds." "The Golden Bird," same symbolic meaning. Reference to this is also in Harold Bayley's book, *The Lost Language of Symbolism.*

Portion sketch K.H.

The Enchanted Stag
The Twin Brothers are found in the tests to be passed in ancient Maya mythology and in Roman, Romulus and Remus, besides the Slavic fable of the twins, "The Twin Brothers" by Wilhelm and Jacob Grimm.

54

Mark—Lion   John—Eagle   Luke—Bull   Matthew—Angel

Sketched by K.H. from Albrecht Dürer's wood carvings.

Sketch by K.H.

Mythological Horse
Head of a Lion, tail of a Serpent from the
Bamberg Apocalypse.

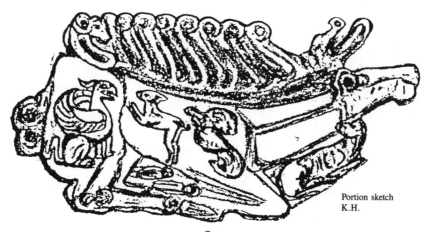

Portion sketch
K.H.

Stag

This animal in sitting position is wrought in gold and is from the Scythian culture
by a Greek artist. One of the magnificent objects brought from Russia to the
Los Angeles County Museum. Upon it, in relief, are sacred symbolic animals:
a Griffin with body of Lion and head and wings of a Phoenix Bird (mythological);
a Deer, Lion, Bull and the head of a Lamb (Ram) atop the back.

55

Portion sketch
K.H.

CHRISTIAN

St. Luke with his animal symbol, the Bull.
One of the Four cardinal points of the Zodiac
in the year period.

Portion sketch
K.H.

Bull and Ram (Lamb), Taurus and Aries. Roman
Forum. Sun between the horns of the Bull—Vernal
Equinox. (Also Chinese Ram).

Sketch K.H.

URATEAN

Sphinx. Head and torso of a
female with body of winged
Lion.

Russian exhibit at Los Angeles
County Museum

56

Portion sketch outline
K.H.

INDIA
Three-legged Toad.
Sketched from *Asiatic Mythology* by J. Haiken.

Sketch K.H.

GREECE
Pegasus—Flying Horse of Chinese and Greek mythology.

57

XIBALBAN MYSTERIES—MAYA
The Bat—Seven Tests of Twin Brothers
Fingernail painting by Kathryn Henry from picture in *The Secret Teachings of All Ages* by Manly P. Hall.

Sketch K.H.

CHINESE AND EUROPEAN
The Unicorn—The Soul
The Unicorn is displayed in many Christian churches and is often
shown in pictures of the Garden of Eden with other animals.

Portion and rough sketch of Michelangelo's human-headed Serpent in the Cistine Chapel, St. Peter's Basilica.

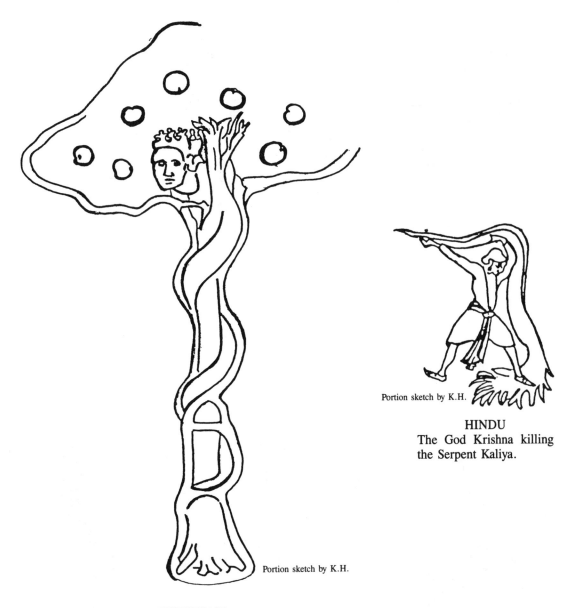

Portion sketch by K.H.

HINDU
The God Krishna killing
the Serpent Kaliya.

Portion sketch by K.H.

CHRISTIAN
Tree—Life, Wisdom and Knowledge. The Apple and human-
headed Serpent.

Besser Chapel, Ulm Cathedral

61

MAYA AND CAMBODIAN SERPENTS

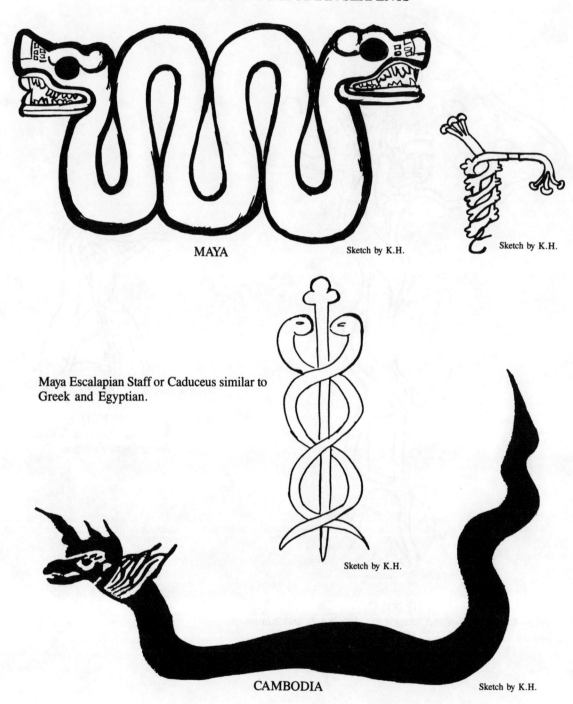

MAYA   Sketch by K.H.

Sketch by K.H.

Maya Escalapian Staff or Caduceus similar to
Greek and Egyptian.

Sketch by K.H.

CAMBODIA   Sketch by K.H.

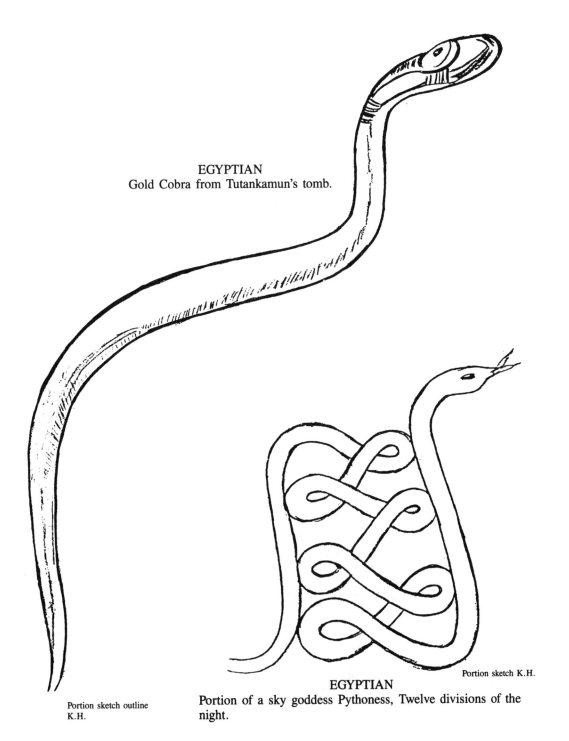

EGYPTIAN
Gold Cobra from Tutankamun's tomb.

Portion sketch K.H.

Portion sketch outline
K.H.

EGYPTIAN
Portion of a sky goddess Pythoness, Twelve divisions of the
night.

63

Portion sketch by K.H.

GREEK—SYRIAN
Ladder and Serpent

Sketch by K.H.

St. Margaret and the Serpent
From Giulio Romano, an outline sketch. Paris,
Louvre.

Huge Serpentine earth mound built by North American Indians in Ohio, USA, by a people who had a golden age between 400 B.C.-400 A.D. John Mitchell, who wrote *The Earth Spirit,* said that there is an egg associated with it, and the huge serpent mound can be seen in its entirety only from the air (see page 82).

Portion sketch from Caravagio's Madonna of the Serpent. Here is sketched only the leg of young Jesus with foot atop the Madonna's, both on the head of the Serpent.

Borghese Gallery, The Vatican.

CHINA

Portion sketch of the elaborate raised Serpent design, the centerpiece of the stairway to the great Temple to Heaven. The Dragon-Serpent being indicative of the solar systems and galaxies of Creation.

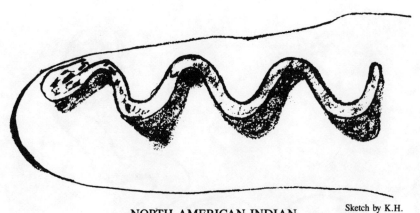

K.H.

Sketch by K.H.

NORTH AMERICAN INDIAN
Copper ceremonial Serpent (on finger).
From the Museum of the Foundation for Illinois Archeology—from photo by Del Baston.

JAPAN
Sketched from gold Serpent in the sky.

Sketch by K.H.

Sketch by K.H.

MAYA
Serpentine Headdress, ear lobes, Oriental
appearance (Mongolian features).
National Museum, Mexico

The smaller goddess of Serpents—a mother
goddess from Gnossos Palace—Minoan.

66

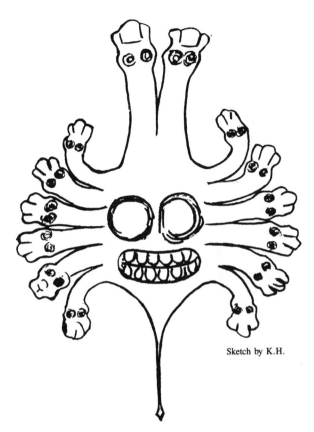

Sketch by K.H.

PERU
Serpentine Headdress

Sketch by K.H.

MAYA
The Serpent is part of the "diving god" motif on the second story
of the palace at Sayil, Yucatan.
Sketched from *The Art of Ancient Mexico* by Groth-Kimball-Feuchtwange.

67

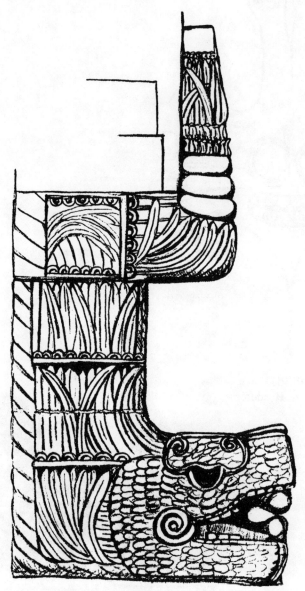

Sketch by K.H.

MAYA
Serpent column in front of the doorway of the Temple
of Tigers. Chichén Itzá, Yucatan.

Sketched from *The Art of Ancient Mexico*
by Groth-Kimball-Feuchtwange.

68

Sketch by K.H.

AZTEC
Snake Goddess
Mother-Goddess of the Serpent Skirt (lower and higher natures)
and Creation. The skull is transitory existence and there are four
palms of hands.

A stone carving pictured in *Renaissance* of Time-Life and a wood carving in
the Library of the Philosophical Research Society, Inc.

Sketch by K.H.

CLASSICAL MAYA
Temple of the Sun at Palenque. Other civilizations have Sun
Temples.

Sketch by K.H.

JAPAN—TAOIST
Fly Whisk (Chauri and Camara), magic
power to drive away demons; whip of
self-mastery.
Metropolitan Museum of Art

Sketch by K.H.

JAPAN
Dragon King of the Sea.
Metropolitan Museum of Art

70

Temples Taipei, Taiwan

Lion Dog

Photos by K.H.

Dragon column

71

CHINA
Photograph by Col. Clarke Johnston
Five-clawed Dragon.

Portion outline sketch
K.H.

JAPAN
Dragon in Billowy Clouds
Here the Dragon is shown with the Sun and was on display for the first time in the United States at the Saint Louis Art Museum and the Seattle Art Museum. The exhibit was brought over by Mr. Kishimoto from Japan—Maruyama, Okyo 1733-1773. From private collection Gifu.

Portion outline sketch by K.H. from very large painted screens behind glass paneled showcases.

73

Portion outline sketch
K.H.

ASSYRIA
Fish-Man

Sketches by K.H.

GREECE
Pegasus, Winged-Horse

CHINA

Top of porcelain altar has Dog on the top of the lid (Dog in Egypt represented faithfulness). Dragons surround the neck of the jar and Lotus Petals surround the bottom of the jar.

Some years ago, while visiting the DeYoung Museum, we saw this in display cases of the Brundage Collection, among many magnificent objects: ceremonial wine vessels, a Bodhisattva and his Toad and, carved in jadeite, Mountains, Trees and Bamboo, a jadeite Sceptre with Lotus decor, a jadeite vase with Phoenix Bird in relief, and an almost transparent jadeite Lotus-petaled bowl.

Avery Brundage Collection, De Young Museum

Portion sketch by K.H.

CHINESE
Five Dragons.
Nelson Gallery, Atkins Museum, Kansas City, Missouri.

Portion sketch by K.H.

Birds and Grapes
Satyr family in a grapevine.
Woodcut by Albrecht Dürer, 1515, Rogers Fund,
1922. Metropolitan Museum of Art.

Portion sketch by K.H.

Chinese Dragon

Sketch K.H.

CHINA
Celestial Dragon.
From Blue and White Plate Collection of Kathryn Henry.

JAPANESE
Dragon swallowing Moon. Three claws is Japanese; five claws, Imperial; Four claws is Chinese; five claws, Mandarin.
Bronze rubbing by Kathryn Henry from collection of K.D.H.

76

Partial sketch K.H.

EGYPTIAN COBRA CROWN
Bust of a princess at the time of Ramses II.
From *Great Museums of the World,* Egyptian Museum, Cairo.

Sketch by K.H.

Selket—Egyptian deity—Scorpion Headdress

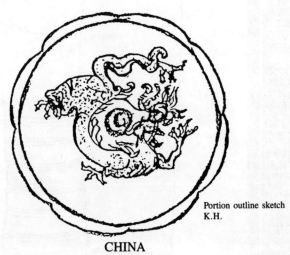

Portion outline sketch
K.H.

CHINA

Mirror with Dragon design. Some mirrors have the Twelve animals
of the Chinese Zodiac in their design bands. Others have human,
monster and Fish; still others have the Four Cardinal Points of the
Zodiac, Tortoise, Tiger, Bird and Dragon, as those of the Western
Zodiac. Mirrors were used in religious ceremonies as with Maya
and Japan. They were used as the Moon, reflection of the Sun,
and connected to the Solar Plexus in magical ceremonies.

Avery Brundage Collection, De Young Museum.

78

EARLY CHRISTIAN, ITALY
Catacomb of St. Callixtus, near Appian Way.
Portion sketches of wall paintings by K.H.

Jonah and the Whale. Appearing to be more a Sea Serpent than a Whale.

The Good Shepherd. The Crook and Flail of the Shepherds, the Cock of the Metallic Vessel (or Iron Pot). The Ram and the Lamb, a Gnostic Cock of Egypt, and the Cock and Pot of China.

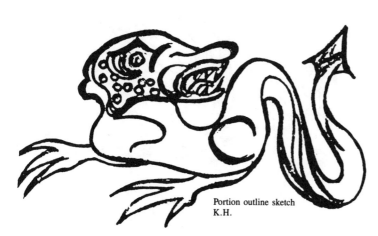

Portion outline sketch
K.H.

Dragon of St. George

Portion sketch by K.H.

ORIENTAL DRAGON
British Museum

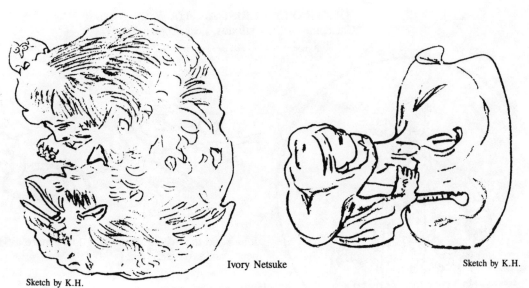

Ivory Netsuke

Sketch by K.H.

Sketch by K.H.

JAPAN

As the legend goes, the long-nosed deity and dancing friend enticed the Sun goddess from her cave.

Metropolitan Museum of Art.

Seven-headed Mythological Creatures and Frogs. An angel shows St. John the River of Paradise from the throne of God and the Lamb; also the Tree of Life bearing Twelve kinds of Fruits and putting them out every month; Twelve times a year.

From The Book of Revelation (Visions of St. John), New Testament. From *Biblical Myths and Mysteries* by Gilbert Thurlow.

Partial sketch K.H.

80

Partial sketch by K.H.

Dragon
From Collection of Mr. Kishimoto of Japan, at Saint Louis Art Museum

Unicorn on disk.

DRAGON DECOR
Taipei, Taiwan

Dragon pillar, Dragon roof-top

Relief Dragon on stone.

82

Sketch by K.H.

Wolf   Bear   Lion   Fox   Hare

Animal Symbolism
Ancient fairy tale of "The Twin Brothers." Slavic, Oriental and European mythology.

Sketch by K.H.

Seven-headed Dragon—Allegory of the Soul

83

PRE-COLUMBIAN
Feathered Serpent Headdress, ear lobe disks.
Sketches of Terra Cotta figures in the Collection of Alvine Higgins by K.H.

In Initiations of Mystery Schools the numbers Three, Seven, Nine and Twelve were significant. Here we have Four sets of Nine.

84

BIRDS

The mystery schools used the symbol of the Bird to indicate great spiritual truths, development of soul, inspiration and beauty; some writers, however, believe that animal symbolism materialized out of animal tribal names. They possibly meant as with the Amerindian, but in this author's opinion, noticing the many symbols that sprang up similarly and almost simultaneously all around the globe and from extensive research, it appears otherwise. Reference from scribes on papyrus, stone carvings, stele, sculpture, monuments, mounds, paintings, etc. indicates that perhaps a central or mother civilization may have passed on a heritage to very early primitive people, a form of knowledge in which animals became symbols of these great truths. Cultures and civilizations developed out of this advanced heritage. This may be the reason archeologists are having such difficulty in determining where the Olmec (preceding the Maya and Aztec of Central America) came from and how they developed. The Maya had folk songs giving testimony that their ancestral heritage came from islands to the east, and the Egyptians on papyrus and stele proclaimed that theirs came from islands to the west. (Refer to Stacey-Judd's *Atlantis, Mother of Empires* and Plato's *Republic.*).

The god Zeus (Greek) or Jupiter (Roman), in ancient mythology, swooped down to earth in the form of an Eagle, taking Gannymede aloft with him to become his cupbearer and then presented him with a Cock; such symbolic gifts should not be thought of (as today) as toys, pets or playthings, but this is often the popular belief and misconception at the present time. The cock represented the advanced soul, not a toy! It is a symbol in Christianity as well.

From Egypt came Freemasonry, and a particular symbol used in their teachings is the Pelican which is feeding its young from the blood of its own breast; also in this emblematic picture is the Rose and a tool (the compass) of the builders (of the soul). In St. Louis, Missouri, there is a Catholic church with a mosaic in the foyer of this same emblem. It stands for the Universe feeding its own creations of itself.

From Egypt, the Gnostics had the Cock as the symbol of the advanced soul, and from early times the Hawk was a sacred symbol of the Sun and of Ra, the Sun god, as well as of Osiris and Horus (offspring of Isis and Osiris), the Trinity. The Sun god Ra wears a Hawk upon his head, the Sun with a Serpent encircling it; Ra is also associated with the Phoenix Sun Bird. Some believe that the Eagle, Peacock and Swan were actually the same as the mythological Phoenix Bird of the Egyptians, Hindus, Orientals, Romans, and Christians, just in different forms.

The Egyptians had the Vulture goddess of death and the Ibis with its long, curved beak belonging to the god Thoth, representing the heart and spirit of the Universe. Christian, Roman, Hindu, and Oriental all revered the Peacock, which represents spiritual qualities of the lofty soul, and the sacred Birds were often shown in the sacred Trees, as in Hindu paintings. The Romans, the American Indians and Greeks gave sacred qualities to the Eagle. The Eagle and Raven were prominent in Indian lore of British Columbian tribes in Canada and of Scandinavia. They represent the highly evolved entities which can fly through the air as a Bird.

The Dove has many meanings. It was a symbol of the ancient Greeks and Romans and also shares a very special place in Christian symbology as the Holy Spirit and also as the Dove of Noah. Because of its gentle qualities, its peaceful nature and its ability to soar and descend, this symbol was used in Freemasonry of the ancient Egyptians. The Cosmic Goose was also used in Egypt and the Orient. Owls and Bats were of witchcraft or wisdom; in the initiation tests of the Maya mysteries a Bat was danger, but in China it was regarded as happiness.

The Owl in ancient Greece was a symbol of Athena, signifying wisdom because of its being bright-eyed, seeing in all directions quickly and seeing and flying in the dark. The Owl was also in Egyptian mythology. Feathers, Angels and winged creatures of all kinds were regarded as spiritual development. Crows, buzzards, condors, and parrots portrayed important significance in various cultures.

The Swan is the symbol of the initiate in the mystery schools, and this beautiful creature is also the subject of sacred symbolic paintings in China, Japan, India, Europe, and in royal crests of the British Isles.

Since the Bird represents the soul of an advanced being, and because the soul takes flight after death, there is this and also a further reason why the Bird applies to the advanced soul. For example, in the civilization of the ancient Maya, the shaman, elevated soul (initiate and adept), is sculptured with one-half the face in ornate design of a Bird while the other half is human. In their practices, ceremonies and tests in the mystery schools, accounts have been recorded as to magical exercises performed by the inner sanctum of priesthoods of all the mystery schools. In the Xibalban mysteries of the ancient Maya, it was recorded by the Spaniards and Jesuits that the shaman could leave the body (his soul and etheric double), at will, and travel through the air (on the astral plane or fourth dimension) and return to the body. Because of this development they were called Bird souls. There are accounts of this from the mystery school of the Egyptian pyramid of Gizeh, as well. In his book, *The Phoenix,* Manly Hall tells of Apollonius performing this feat in order to save his life from the Roman tribunal.

The Falcon and Eagle are also in Chinese symbolism; the Eagle for its virtues of boldness and keen vision; the Hawk in Turkestan for its authority. Finally there is the mythological Thunderbird of the American Indian. This parallels the Phoenix Bird of the Orient as being an adept or a superior being. Birds in general in antiquity were considered a creative aspect or a symbol of creative forces. The American Indian also used the Eagle; the Maya and people in Bali, the Owl.

In Egyptian mythology, Birds symbolized were the Hawk, mythological Phoenix, the Goose

86

(Seb), the Ibis, Falcon, Pelican, and Vulture. A primeval mound and a celestial Goose were ancient Egyptian symbols shown in *Egyptian Mythology* by Richard Patrick, who described the Ibis who laid the Cosmic Egg! Even though the Falcon is the Bird of the delta deity of Egypt, light from the Eyes indicates a deeper meaning. The Heron of the Egyptians was also used in symbolism the same as the Oriental Phoenix, the mythological Bird.

Portion sketch by K.H.

JAPAN
Swans and Lotus.

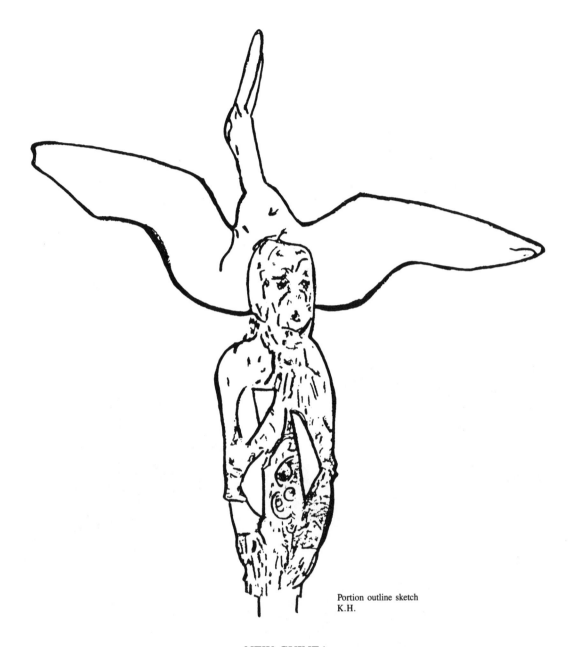

Portion outline sketch
K.H.

NEW GUINEA
Soul Bird-Man
Washington University Collection, St. Louis, Missouri. Wood
carving. This is also in the Saint Louis Art Museum.

EGYPT
Ducks and Goose
Painting from tomb of Itab from *Great Museums of the World*, Egyptian Museum, Cairo.

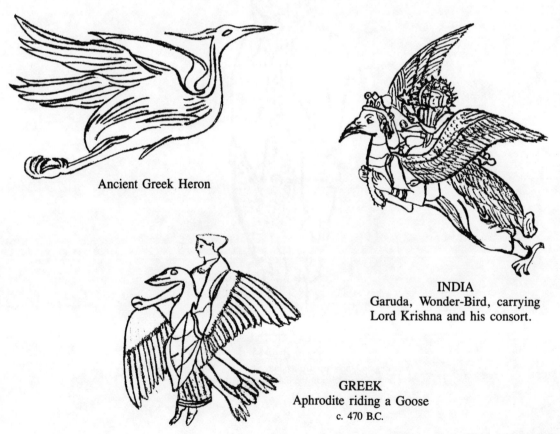

Ancient Greek Heron

INDIA
Garuda, Wonder-Bird, carrying
Lord Krishna and his consort.

GREEK
Aphrodite riding a Goose
c. 470 B.C.

Partial sketches by K.H.

Sketch by K.H.

CHINA

Painted in gold and silver on black. From lacquered box of Kathryn Henry
Collection.

91

Bird and Blossoms   By Marjean Von Engeln.

Photo by Don Dwiggins.

Portion outline sketch
K.H.

GREECE
Man riding Cock
From *Athenian Red Figure Vases, The Archaic Period,*
by John Boardman.

92

CHINA
Bodhisattva Ivory Headdress
Kathryn Henry Collection

CHINA
Jade Birds
Kathryn Henry Collection

CHINA
Dragon on Vase
Kathryn Henry Collection

CHINA
Bird on Lacquer Box
Kathryn Henry Collection
Photos by Clarke Johnston.

93

Rooster-Bird
The Cock and Plum Blossoms. Cock greets the dawn, symbol of
Sun, Chinese and Gnostics. Cock's comb represents pineal gland
as does Indian feather, pine cone, ureas of Egypt, etc.
From octagonal plate, collection of Kathryn Henry.

Phoenix Bird and Chrysanthemums
Advanced Soul and the Wise Ones.
Original drawing, Oriental style, by K.H.

95

Cranes

By Marjean Von Engeln.

96

Rubbings by K.H.

JAPAN
Bamboo and Birds
From Kathryn Henry Collection.

97

CHINA
Bronze rubbing by K.H.
From the collection of Kathryn Henry

CHINA
Ching Dynasty Plate
From the collection of Kathryn Henry

CHINA
Phoenix Bird, carved ivory
Kathryn Henry collection.
Photo by Clarke Johnston

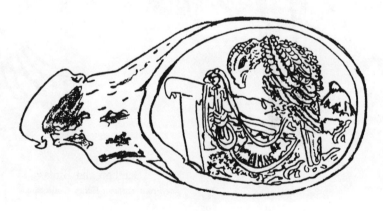

JAPAN
Dream symbols—good fortune. Soul-Falcon, Egg.
Ivory Netsuke. Mt. Fuji. Metropolitan Museum of Art.

Sketches by K.H.

Gliding Gull

Photo by Don Dwiggins

Photo by Don Dwiggins

Bird of the Pacific

100

Portion sketch K.H.

Bird Mask
Malanggen, long-eared helmet mask.
New Ireland.
Saint Louis Art Museum

Sketch by K.H.

NAVAJO INDIAN
Sand painting. Paintings in lovely
colors were used in healing
ceremonies.
Sketch from collection of Kathryn Henry.

Portion sketch K.H.

AMERICAN INDIAN
Bird ceremonial dance. From
Shebala.

101

Birds and Rabbits
The Soul and aspects concerning the Moon.
Original drawings by K.H. Oriental style.

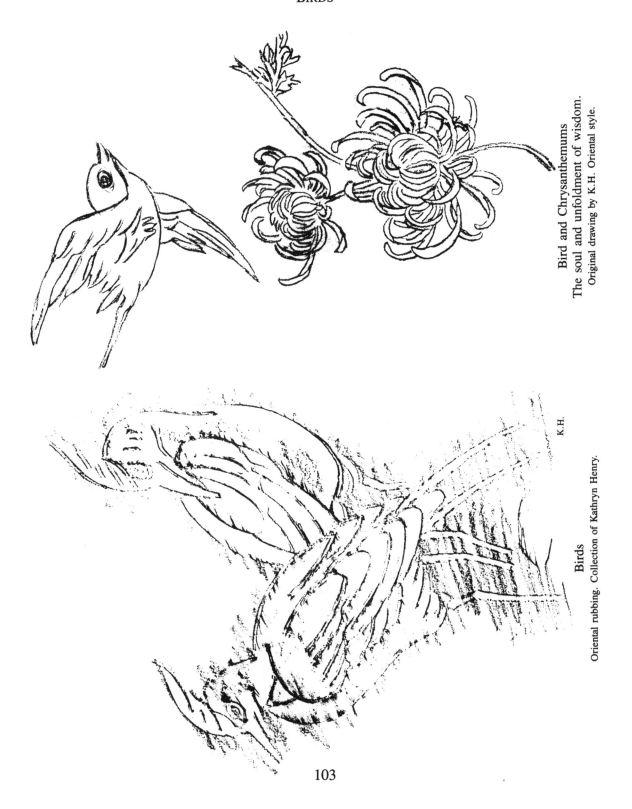

Bird and Chrysanthemums
The soul and unfoldment of wisdom.
Original drawing by K.H. Oriental style.

K.H.

Birds
Oriental rubbing. Collection of Kathryn Henry.

103

Bee, Bird and Blossom
Wisdom, soul and unfoldment
Original drawing by K.H. Oriental style.

Sketch by K.H.

JAPAN
Hawk
There are several meanings to this symbol.
Ivory netsuke. Metropolitan Museum of Art.

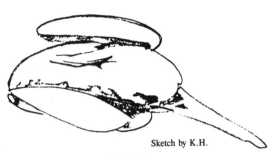

Sketch by K.H.

JAPAN
Kingfisher Bird
Ivory netsuke. Metropolitan Museum of Art.

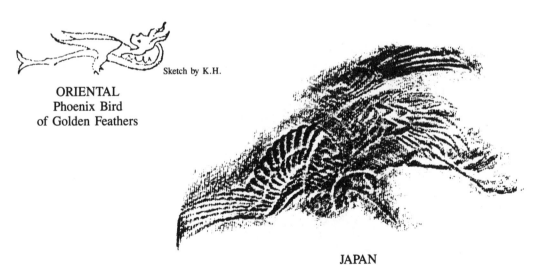

Sketch by K.H.

ORIENTAL
Phoenix Bird
of Golden Feathers

JAPAN
Bird rubbing by K.H. Collection of Kathryn Henry.

105

Portion sketch by K.H.

FRANCE

Mid-tenth century. Ivory comb of St. Gauzelin.

From *Art of the Dark Ages* by Magnus Backes and Regine Dolling: "The motif of vine leaves, rising from a vessel decorated with birds, probably doves, recalls Carolingian and early Christian symbolism: the human soul (birds) feeds on the sacrificial gifts of Christ (wine and chalice). . . . It has been assumed that the comb was exported from Fatimid Egypt or copied from a Fatimid work."

Portion sketch by K.H.

GERMANY

Middle Ages, resembling Egyptian.
Eagle fibula.

106

TREES, MOUNTAINS AND RIVERS

TREES

The symbol of Trees concerns the Tree of Life, of Wisdom and Knowledge, of Time and Destiny, of Good and Evil, evil being the absence of good or God. The Tree shows man's development in character or soul and in symbolism is the spinal cord in many religions. Rivers symbolize the spinal cord, also, in all the Seven great world religions.

The Oak Tree was sacred to the Greek god Zeus in mythology and to the ancient Romans. The sacred Oak Grove was a ceremonial place of the Druid priests (along with their Stonehenge monumental zodiacal circles).

There is the Sephiroth Tree of the ancient Hebrew in the sacred Cabala with its extremely complicated diagrams of a highly technical mathematical, astrological/astronomical significance, representing in geometry, trigonometry and calculus a developed system of the Universe and man; a religious impact that was one of the greatest instructional documents ever to have been struck down or written by man—a truly magnificent work.

The beautiful Evergreen or Christmas Tree of the Christians is the symbol of everlasting life, the Evergreen being the highest form of plant life, remaining green throughout the cold of winter weather. The heart of man is the area of the seed atom of the spirit of God, the flame of God-given energy and love. In Christianity it is the flame in the heart. The lights on the Tree symbolize this, as does the golden pagoda in the heart of the Oriental. The Palm is also one of the Christian Tree symbols.

In Egyptian symbolism, it is the Acacia (an Evergreen) and Palm. In the Hindu, it is the Acacia, Palm, Bodhi, Plantain, and Mango Trees. The Bodhi or Bo Tree, under which (Prince Sidhartha) Lord Gautama Buddha rested when he received his illumination. is the Tree of Enlightenment and the way of moderation, the middle path, eliminating the extremes. The Tree of the spine and the Seven chakras are connected to the Seven original planetary bodies.

In the Minoan civilization of Crete, the Greek isle, the Trees of symbolism are Olive, Cypress and Date Palm (sacred in the Bronze Age). The Palm is also a symbolic Tree of Syria.

In the culture of the ancient Maya civilization of Central America, it is the Calabash Tree. As the allegory goes, upon one of its branches was a head which spat upon the Virgin princess, who immaculately conceived twin boys as a result. The boys had to pass Seven planetary tests in order to be initiated into the Xibalban mysteries (the Seven original planets of the solar system), as previously accounted.

There is the Yggdrasil Tree of Scandinavia with the Eagle and the Serpent which is the huge world Ash Tree created by All-Father. During the Middle Ages there was the Tree of Alchemy. With the Chinese, Babylonians and Persians it was the Acacia Tree, and in the Garden of Eden it is the Tree of Life where the Serpent twines around with its human head.

In the Bible, in the Song of Solomon, chapter 2, verse 3, it is written, "As an Apple Tree among the Trees of the wood, so is my love among the sons," and Jason of the Golden Fleece is pictured on a Boat with Dove and Tree. Noah, Boat, Dove, and Olive Branch are featured in the allegory.

There is still another symbolic Tree of the ancient Egyptians, and that is the Sycamore, sacred to the Cow goddess, Hathor.

Haiti also had its sacred Tree. In a recent voodoo ceremony in Haiti, the priest in a baptism mentioned the Rosicrucians, the Master Masons and St. John and then proceeded with a fire ritual.

The Christmas Tree celebration in ancient Rome was the Roman Saturnalia (ceremony to Saturn), the planet that is associated with Father Time, the Scythe, the Reaper, and the Hour Glass. This is the symbolism of problems, lessons to learn and the Teacher.

The Christmas Tree was tradition in the 1880s, accompanied by Father Christmas who was once Odin or Woden of the Scandinavians. The Norse goddess (Scandinavia) entered and left by way of chimneys, and the people decorated the Fir Tree or Evergreen in celebration.

An East-West parallel given by Manly Hall in regard to Santa Claus conveys that he is supposed to live at the North Pole, and in this tale it is a bleak and inhospitable region where it is dark for nearly half of the year. In ancient India, the great polar mountain of the earth was Meru or Sumuro, the axis of the world and the abode of the immortals. From this mountain, streams of life made all the world fertile and from treasure palaces sent forth streams of blessings upon all living creatures.

MOUNTAINS

Mountains are used in all the great world religions signifying the head or brain; the development of the mental faculties enables the spirit to better manifest since it is the most potent part of body.

There are Mt. Ararat, Mt. Sinai and the Mount of Olives in the Bible. There are Mt. Meru of the Hindus and Mt. Fuji of Japan. The Volcano Mountain of Hawaii is inhabited by Pele, the fire goddess of Kilauea.

Both Buddha and Christ gave their sermons "on the Mount."

Original painting
by K.H.

CHRISTIAN
Evergreen Tree

109

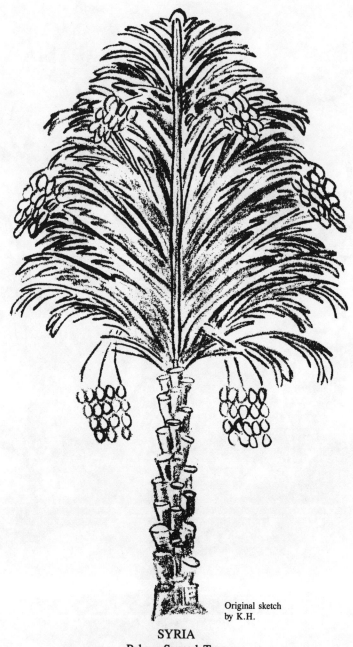

Original sketch
by K.H.

SYRIA
Palm—Sacred Tree
Also Christian.

Original sketch
by K.H.

The Human Tree
Inspired by Manly P. Hall from *The Secret Teachings of All Ages.*

111

TREES

The Christian Holy Family is sometimes shown sitting under the Oak Tree, which was also sacred to the Druids. There is a partridge in a Pear Tree, and the Japanese Shinto still celebrate the Sacred Tree Ceremony.

Sketch by K.H.

MAYA, CENTRAL AMERICA
Tau Cross in form of Tree with Bird

Sketch by K.H.

INDIA
Acacia Tree—Sacred
with Birds—Soul

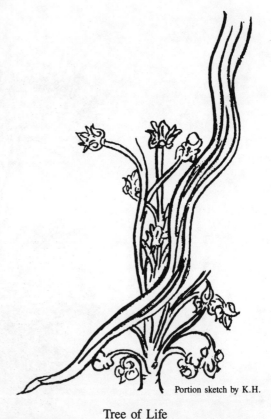

Portion sketch by K.H.

Tree of Life
River flowing from throne of God upon which sits the Messiah giving the Blessing. From St. John in Revelations (22:17): "And whosoever will, let him take the water of life freely," and Jesus: "Blessed is the man who has suffered, he has found Life." The Tree of Life is also pictured in the Garden of Eden.

112

Pine bough and Mountain
Everlasting Life and the Spirit of God in the heart.
Original drawing by K.H., Oriental style.

Portion sketch by K.H.

MAYA

Tree of Life, Wisdom and Knowledge with the head of the Feathered Serpent and skull below (our transitory existence) flanked by two priests in feathered headdresses.

Sketched from photo of copy in the National Museum of Anthropology, Mexico. Photo was taken by Ed Higgins.

114

JAPAN
Bamboo Trees
Kikue Atkins oil painting.

115

CHINA
Tree branch and Mountain
Brush painting by Cheryl Neunkirk

Kathryn Henry Collection
Rubbing by K.H.

JAPAN
Tree and Sacred Mt. Fuji San

116

JAPAN
Tree, Mountain and Moon
Private collection Gifu.

Portion outline sketch
by K.H.

117

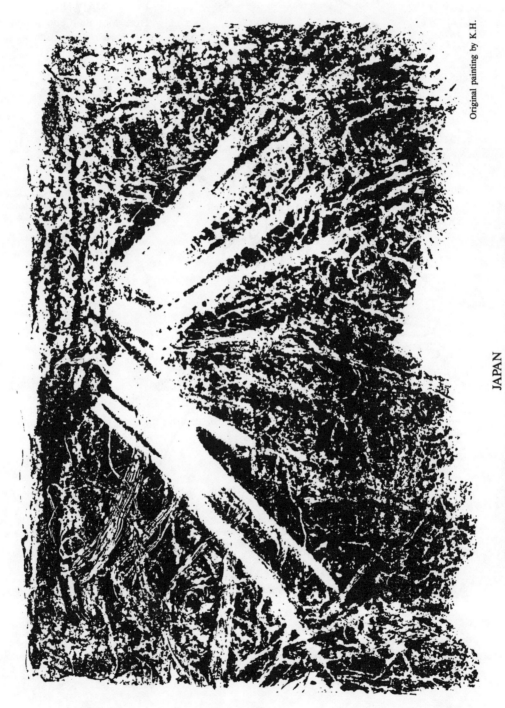

Original painting by K.H.

JAPAN
Painting of Mt. Fuji. Mountains are in all the great world religions.

118

FLOWERS

With Flower symbolism, the idea was to express the meaning of growth, the opening of blossoms with unfolding petals becoming the various states of consciousness and the unfoldment of the soul. In western religions, it is the Rose, the Daisy and the Lily whereas in Oriental and Egyptian symbology it is the Lotus. The Lotus born are also from China, and being seated on the Lotus throne is being seated in universal law after many incarnations from the wheel of rebirth. In Japan, the revered flowers are the Lotus and Chrysanthemum. Oriental philosophy also divides all of humanity into four categories or types of plant life; Plum or Apricot correlates to the artists, the Orchid to the aristocrat, Bamboo to the labor or working class because at the time of an earthquake people would seek safety in the bamboo groves where the roots grew tight, giving protection underfoot. This is analogous to the stability needed from the working class of people upon which others may build. The Chrysanthemum belonged to the philosophers or the wise few.

We must look behind the symbols to discover the purpose and importance of symbolic sacred art. The mystery schools of all ancient civilizations throughout history gave us cultural heritage from which we can realize our full potential, as well as reasons for existence in the Universe. By living a life of particular disciplines we might evolve greatly in the course of time. By learning the true meanings behind the symbolism and by living the life described, the mystery schools believed that in this event the progressions of the human life-wave could be greatly expanded.

The study of the meanings of symbols of sacred art in no way interferes with or opposes anyone's religious or philosophical beliefs, but instead enhances the understanding of one's own faith. The parallels, similarities and identities are astounding.

In the Song of Solomon from the Bible, it says, "I am the Rose of Sharon," "the Lilly of the Valley," and there is mention of all these: apples, apple trees, cedar and cypress, turtledoves, figs, vines, gazelles (deer), pomegranates, and honeycombs (the symbol of mystery schools).

Portion sketch by K.H.

CHRISTIAN
Lily

CHINA
Peonies and Bird
National Palace Museum, Taiwan.
Photo by Clarke Johnston.

From Nature
Photo by Chandler Kennedy

120

JAPAN
Flowers—Chrysanthemums, Plum Blossom
Trees—Evergreen, Bamboo
and Bird

Japanese Sumi painting by K.H. Lessons from T. Makami.

121

Chrysanthemums
In Japan these flowers represent the very learned wise ones.
Original drawing by K.H., Oriental style.

122

THE SUN, SUN DISKS AND MASKS

In antiquity, the lives of all the great world teachers were told in a solar myth. Both Ra and Osiris were Sun gods of Egypt, and Horus was the son of both. Christ, Buddha, Mithras, and Apollo were shown as Sun gods. In the Vatican there is a ceiling mosaic in the tomb of the Julii where Christ is the Sun god surrounded by grape vines (signifying regeneration), riding in a chariot (as Apollo) and driving the white horses. This is in *Treasures of the Vatican* by Marizio Calvese (1962). In Florence, Italy, at the palace of the de' Medici family, there is a mural painted on a wall showing Christ driving his chariot across the sky as the Sun god.

The temples of Solomon were built in the style of Grecian architecture, having the same dimensions as the Dionysian temple of Greece. In deciphering the name "Solomon," we find this:

SOL-OM-ON=the Sun (old Sol)

Solomon is the Sun lord of the universe and Je-Ho-Va=lord of the universe. Several cultures and races have contributed to this symbol. Catholic chants have in them the sound of the "OM" as in the Russian Orthodox chants and the "AUM" of the Hindus, the "OM" representing the sound of the energy power of this Universe. Solomon is Sun energy.

Since legends and myths have often been woven around real people and historical events, so Solomon in the Bible represents the Sun. The Queen of Sheba was said to be the daughter of the Sun. One of the purposes of the myth may have been to show that what the center of the solar system creates has always been a part of the solar system and is nourished by it, as with the Pelican feeding its young of its own blood, as described in Freemasonry and Catholicism mentioned earlier.

In Egypt, the Sun god, Ra, son of Nut, the Sky god, battled a Serpent at night. The Sun god is also represented as a Lion, Cat and Falcon with a solar disk on his head, and he is crossing the heavens in his Sky Boat.

Through centuries, statues of great souls have been sculptured, carved, painted, and cast in flowing robes. This is the flow of universal energy and the continuous working of universal law. The flow of the Sun's energy and its deflected rays from the planets are important factors in time-space and in astrological and astronomical mathematics.

American, Canadian and Central American Indians worshipped the Sun, the central power of the solar system, and they wore Sun masks representing god, the power, in their sacred ceremonies.

The Sun's symbols are the diamond, gold, the sunflower, and the daisy (symbolizing the day's eye).

George Ferguson in his *Signs and Symbols in Christian Art* says of the Sun and Moon that the Sun is symbolic of Christ and that this interpretation was based on the prophecy of Malachi 4:2: "But unto you that fear my name shall the Sun of righteousness arise with healing in his wings." He said that the Sun and Moon are used as attributes of the Virgin Mary, referring to the "woman clothed with the Sun, and the Moon under her feet" (Revelations 12:1) and that the Sun and Moon are often represented in scenes of the crucifixion to indicate the sorrow of all creation at the death of Christ. Humanity crucifies its higher self until it attains illumination, so say all the great teachers of world religions.

The Sun god of Greece was called Helios and sometimes Apollo, Hercules and Perseus. He was always the offspring of Jupiter in the allegory, king of all the gods, and was always Virgin born! Oral E. Scott tells of this in *The Stars in Myth and Fact,* and Manly Hall in *Twelve World Teachers* enumerates twenty-five allegorical, immaculately conceived births. In *The Secret Teachings of All Ages,* he explains the universal solar cosmic myth that is in all the ancient religions and philosophies of all civilizations. This myth involves the Four points in the earth's rotation; hence sacred feast days fall close together in the different religions of the different races.

Robert Graves in his *The Greek Myths* speaks of mounds representing the Sun and Moon having been built of sea shells, quartz and white marble. The ancient Hebrew honored the Moon with mounds made of white sea shells. In Greek mythology, the Sun was subordinate to the Moon until the later Greek myths when they became reversed.

About twenty-five years ago in the highlands of Peru, the natives told an explorer and friend that the Mask represented God. Whoever was high in esteem and was qualified to wear the mask was receiving the wisdom of God. This is true in Tibet, Mexico, Africa, and other civilizations just as the Headdress and Staff.

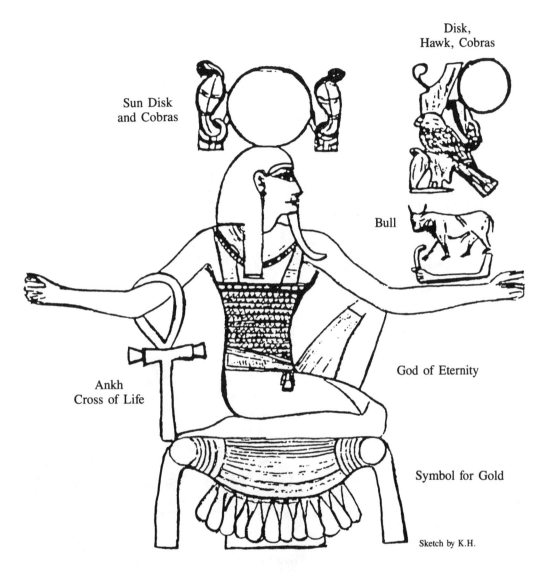

EGYPT
Sketch portions of chair from tomb of Tutankhamun.
Cairo Museum

125

Portion outline sketch
K.H.

MEXICO—PRE-COLUMBIAN
Sun-like face. "The Word," creation. Open mouth with
protruding tongue.

Morton May Collection, St. Louis Art Museum.

ETRUSCAN
Gorgon's head. Approximately 500 B.C.
Open mouth and serpents.

Portion outline sketch
K.H.

126

Portion sketch by K.H.

ITALY
Creation—The Word. Open mouth face and wings on breastplate of Guliano de' Medici.
National Gallery of Art, Washington, D.C.

127

Portion sketch by K.H.

EGYPT—LION
Open mouth, protruding tongue. (Significant checkerboard design.)

Tutankhamon's tomb, portion of vessel.

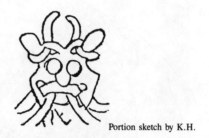

Portion sketch by K.H.

Viking Stone
Horns and open mouth

Portion sketch by K.H.

Portion of Aztec calendar (originally Maya). Open mouth, The Word, creation—the Sun. Note squares, circles and angles.

128

Portion sketch K.H.

AZTEC

Stone Disc—Sun God

The face of the Sun God resembles a Lion. A knife issues from the mouth as the Sword from the mouth of the Christian Messiah with the Sun radiating behind him, from St. John's Revelation. The sword and knife sever man from materiality to becoming spiritual. There is a Serpentine motif in the center and the tail of the Feathered Serpent at the top of the disk. He is surrounded by skulls of the underworld symbolic of our transitory existence, as in Christianity.

129

ITALY
The Mouth of Truth
Creation
The Word
Sun Disk
From the Church of St. Mario in Cosmedin, Rome.

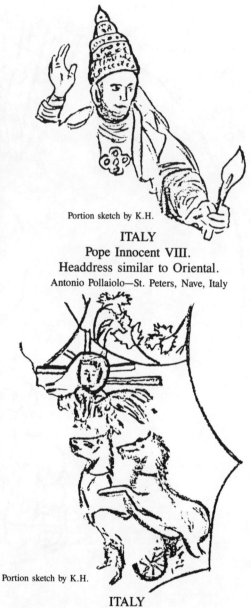

Portion sketch by K.H.

ITALY
Pope Innocent VIII.
Headdress similar to Oriental.
Antonio Pollaiolo—St. Peters, Nave, Italy

Portion sketch by K.H.

ITALY

That which remains of a mosaic—Christ as the
Sun God in his chariot going across the sky as
did the Greek God, Apollo.

From *The Mosaics of Rome* by Walter Oakes Hott. In this
book is a mosaic of the Crucifixion with the scroll growing
from the base of the Cross along with an animal grazing and
a coiled reddish Serpent, as is the Serpent Kundalini in the
Hindu teachings coiled at the base of the spine. There are
also Seven Doves on the Cross.

130

Portion sketch by K.H.

HOPI, AMERINDIAN
Sun God, Kachina Doll

Bull

Sketch from Durer woodcut.
K.H.

From hymns and the Bible, Christianity as-
sists in the mystery that this is the "woman
clothed with the Sun and the Moon under
her feet and upon her head a crown of
twelve stars." (Rev. 12:1). She stands for the
Holy Spirit. The crowned bull has the living waters flowing from his mouth. Ma-
donnas with crowns of stars, clothed in the
Sun, the Moon under their feet, are still
to be found today in Switzerland, Germany,
Austria, and elsewhere.

Monstrance of the Cross and Sun, carried
by Father Marquette, French explorer.
Raphael also painted Sun Disk.
St. Louis Globe-Democrat.

Madonna and Child. The infant holds a
pomegranate or apple.
Saint Louis Art Museum

132

Sketch by K.H.

JAPAN
Mask
Metropolitan Museum of Art

133

SAVIORS, WORLD VIRGINS, TRINITIES, AND TRIADS, CROSSES AND LADDERS, ALLEGORIES AND DEITIES ALL-SEEING EYE

SAVIORS, WORLD VIRGINS, TRINITIES, AND TRIADS

In the Christian religion, the world Virgin is Mary, who has immaculately conceived from the Holy Ghost, giving birth to the Savior Jesus. At another time in ancient Greece, Pythagoras, a great philosopher and teacher, was also recorded to have been immaculately conceived, as the allegory goes, and was born, as was Jesus, while his mother was on a journey. Some say these two were actually born in Syria in towns not far distant from one another.

The crook and the flail were symbolic instruments of the shepherds (great world teachers) used in Egypt and borrowed by the Christians.

The mother of the Persian Savior, Manas, was called the "widow," and, as mentioned under Trees, in the ancient Maya civilization the Virgin princess conceived by being spat upon by a head hanging from a sacred Tree. The Tree was the Calabash or the Ceiba with foliage extending to the sky and roots to the underworld, according to the allegorical legend of the Xibalban mysteries. From Mother Earth come the words "mammal," "mama" and the Hebrew name of "Miriam" or "Mary."

In observing the statue of the Virgin of Paris, the infant is holding a pomegranate or apple which has a deep meaning, and he is not just "playing with the mother's veil," as stated in the caption, but is a "veiled account" of the teacher penetrating the veil of the mysteries, just as the veil of the Egyptian world mother, Isis, was penetrated by souls having evolved to an elevated state. There is a statue of the Virgin of Paris in the Saint Louis Art Museum.

There are mother goddesses recorded from Sumeria, 2700-2500 B.C., and in Austria there is a mother symbol which is a primitive carving about 15,000-20,000 B.C. that is supposed to be capable of magic.

In the allegories of divine Saviors, the sages of China were said to have been born of a Virgin, like the Chaldean Savior Oannes (under Fish), with the Serpent-like Fish body and head of a man. Sages were pictured as Dragons and Lions, as mentioned earlier, as well as resembling a Fish.

The birth announcement of a sage in China was heralded by a scaled sacred animal with one horn on the forehead (Unicorn). In Christianity, an angel appeared to the Virgin for the announcement. An Elephant on a cloud announced the tidings of the birth of the great Hindu teacher, Lord Gautama Buddha, who was immaculately conceived to his mother, Maya. Egypt's Trinity was Isis, Osiris and Horus. Isis (Virgin spirit and lessons of Mother Earth) gave birth to Horus (the soul and great world teacher), having been impregnated by Osiris

135

(the Holy Spirit). The chest myth of this Trinity is somewhat similar to that of Moses in the bullrushes.

Ancient Greece also had its Trinities and world mothers (refer to Plato, Pythagoras and Proclus). Hinduism had its three-gods-in-one deity, and the Saviors of Tibet were called Lotus born. Ancient Peru had a Trinity. The Christian Trinities are (1) Father, Son and Holy Ghost, (2) Holy Spirit, Virgin Spirit (world mother) or Mary, mother of Jesus, the teacher.

CROSSES

The Aztec culture, in their religious symbolism, had an "X" type of Cross which is shown on an ancient Codex painted on linen-like material. The hero is upon the Cross, and a little gold man with a little gold bow and arrow shoots the arrow into the right side of the hero, into the liver area. Manly Hall has this Codex. In the mystery schools of antiquity, they describe this area as being the part of the body where the seed atom of man's lower emotions is located. When piercing that part of the body, the symbolism is enacting the severing of the lower nature from the higher nature. This is also the Christian and Buddhist teaching. We find this in Greek mythology, the higher self corresponding to Emerson's oversoul and St. Paul's hierarchy (the hope and glory within) or the Christ consciousness in this phase of Christianity.

In the Egyptian initiation of the mysteries, the neophyte or the one being initiated was also attached to an "X" Cross. Another Egyptian Cross, in their symbolic and sacred paintings, is the Cross Ansata, the Cross of Life, the key or Ankh. They were carried by the advanced souls (initiate-priest rulers) and deities. In the later dynasties, the priesthood or pharaohs were not nearly as advanced as in the earlier ones.

The Ankh is found among the Maya and Quiche relics throughout Central America and is carved on the backs of Easter Island figures as seen in the British Museum and photographed in *National Geographic*.

The Maya Cross has the crucifixion of Quetzalcoatl on an X Cross; he was the messenger of the Sun deity. Some say the classical culture was at its peak in mid-eighth century A.D., but others believe it to have been centuries earlier.

The immortal Christna of India was tied to a Cross-shaped Tree, and there was also an Oriental drawing of a crucifixion in space where there were light rays extending from the head instead of a crown of thorns; the Savior was suspended in space as though on a Cross, but actually was not. Marks were on the hands and feet, but no nails, these places being areas where the vortices (like circular currents) are located in the human body, as testified by ancient philosophers. Manly Hall quotes J. P. Lundy in his *Monumental Christianity* as saying, "Can it be the Victim-man or the Priest and Victim both in one, of the Hindu mythology, who offered himself a sacrifice before the worlds were?" The Tau Cross was found among the Druids, Egyptians and the Masonic Order. The people of Jerusalem used it, as told by the prophet Ezekiel, as a symbol of liberation.

The Cross and Swastika were found among the Apache North American Indians and other Amerindian tribes. The Japanese, too, used the Cross symbol of the Swastika.

On the Tibetan Mandala (sacred object of concentration and meditation) is laid out the Cross, the symbol of heaven.

Then there is the triple Tau Cross of Freemasonry (from Egypt) and the double and triple Crosses of both Masonic and Roman Catholic symbolism.

In the Christian religion, Christ on the Cross has been pierced in the right side (liver area) by a soldier's spear. The plunging or "shaking of the spear" has been associated with the pen name (Shakespeare), which is another subject and a long story.

The circle with the Cross within it is the symbol of the earth, the symbol of the Universe and man, and it is called many names. It is the two equinoxes and two solstices and is the Sacred Four that Oral Scott talks about in connection with Four fixed stars (Suns of other solar systems). He related that about 5,000 years ago these Four stars were seated on the Cardinal Points of the heavens, Aldebaran on the Vernal Equinox, Regulus on the Summer Solstice, Antares on the Autumnal Equinox, and Fomalhaut on the Winter Solstice. They were believed to watch over the great Cross of the Heavens, each ruling its part of the day and sky in royal splendor; thus, they were venerated as "Guardians of the Sky."

The Sacred Four or Four primary forces are represented by the Four cosmic beings, the Lion, Bull, Cherub (man), and Serpent, which symbols Matthew, Mark, Luke, and John took as their particular symbols, these disciples having an understanding of the Universe. According to James Churchward, these four powers were called:

> The Four Great Primary Forces
> The Sacred Four
> The Four Builders of the Universe (Freemasonry)
> The Four Great Pillars of the Universe
> The Four Genii
> Elohim and Seraphim of the Hebrews
> Archangels of Christianity and Mohammedans
> The Four Great Ones
> The Four Powerful Ones
> The Four Strong Ones
> The Four Great Kings
> The Four Great Maharajas
> The Four Great Architects (Freemasonry)
> The Four Great Geometricians

The Sun, when crossing at the Autumnal Equinox, forms a Cross or "crucifixion" where it remains at its lowest point for Three days in the "tomb." The tomb is also the skeleton wherein resides the soul, the bones or stones, states Manly Hall. Bika Reed said that when

Christ rides the ass, the symbol of the Sun and the ass together make a double being of opposite forces forming a Cross in human form. This is the same idea as the crucifying of the higher nature while we still remain in lower character or soul growth. Another Cross form is man himself with outstretched arms, the form from which many churches have been built.

Scientists today are attempting to explore the differences and similarities between the Biblical and scientific thought concerning creation of the world from the Book of Genesis, but this would seem to be a lost cause and waste of effort since all the bibles of the different religions of the various civilizations were mainly and mostly written in allegory. It seems that in our Bible there is the symbology of states of consciousness labeled Hades or hell (hell-fire and damnation) through which alchemists and Christian saints alike had to pass, underworlds like those in Greek mythology, as the underworld of Pluto, which we are passing through today with the many trials and tribulations of earth life. The Egyptian allegory shows the condemned souls stoking the fires of Osiris and also lying in the Lake of Fire. The Hindu god, Yama, ruled over the underworld or earth life, as did Pluto.

The Tau Cross or "T" has been found in Hindu symbolism, Chinese, Chaldean, Inca, Quiche-Maya, Egyptian, and Hebrew symbology. This is also the Cross of Abraham with a Serpent entwined over it.

Many fine and beautiful books are being published on antiquity, but it is sad to see the lack of correct interpretation and the unfortunate literal acceptance of allegories, symbols and mythology, simply because of inadequate research.

THE LADDER

As the allegory relates, Quetzalcoatl, the Savior of the ancient Maya civilization, descended to earth on a Ladder. The Hopi, North American Indians, as told by G. S. Multen (1980) in the *Spider Woman Stories* (the legends of the Hopi Indians), had a Ladder in their mythology, too. The great world hero goes to the underground Cave of the goddess of earth (Spider Woman). Multen compares this to the Delphic Oracle and priestesses where the Serpents dwelt, in the Grecian practice. This does differ somewhat, however, in that the people made this a literal ceremonial procedure, not just the legend. The Ladder in Hopi mythology represents the 33 tests of initiation involving the spinal column and the growth of an individual to become a great world hero, as in the Freemasonry of the ancient Egyptians.

The Seven underground tests of the ancient Maya twin heroes, representing the Seven original planets involved with the Seven chakras of the spinal column, are like the subterranean tests in the pyramid of Gizeh in Egypt and those of Plato in the Greek mystery schools.

The Greek and other mystery schools taught in their allegories that earth life is full of tests for character growth. The earth life is the underworld ruled by Pluto, as explained earlier, who absconds with Persephone, daughter of Ceres, until revivement once more in the upper

138

regions (actually the spirit world). This upper world is ruled by Ceres, an earth mother goddess.

The late Marc Edmund Jones and James Pryse, who wrote *The Apocalypse Unsealed,* spoke of Revelations 6:1-8 where Four seals were horsemen who then progressed along the central nervous system, up the Ladder of the spine as the soul gradually developed.

In the Gnostic and early Christian mysteries, Manly Hall revealed that the Ladder was one of the principal symbols used in meditative discipline relating to emanations and the polarization of Two forms, spirit and matter, matter being the lowest state of spirit (gross or dense spirit). He said the Ladder symbolized a pattern of levels of emanations from the divine power coming down in waves, one after another, like the tides along the shore bringing divine light down into the abyss of matter, which Jacob Boehme called it.

Quoting Mr. Hall, "Gnosticism taught that man's growth was a sequential unfoldment of his own inner life on ascending levels. From below upward he had, through regeneration, to reach the central point of himself, which was the luminosity of his own soul. It was in his own soul that his body ascending met his spirit descending, and this union produced the Divine Being within him." We are reminded again of St. Paul when he spoke of the "Christ within," the hope and glory. In the Hebrew alphabet, the letters are all tipped with the flame of God's spiritual energy.

Returning again to Manly Hall, he said, "The Gnostic School borrowed from Egypt, Greece and the Cabala (ancient Hebrew), and being emanationists, their philosophy of life was built upon the Mithric Ladder of the Persians and Greeks. There is Homer's cave of the nymphs (in reference to all underground mythologies) and the mysterious Symbolic Ladder that is nearly always shown leaning against the Cross at the bringing down of the body of the Christ from the Cross. The Ladder in Egypt tipped so that the top of it pointed toward the constellation of the Seven Stars, the great Bear, and it was the symbol of initiation into the mysteries and the heavenly ascent of the human soul." The Bear is shown in stained glass windows of the Christian church. The Vikings, too, used the Bear as a symbol. The Ladder was also a symbol of aspiration besides that of soul growth. This is the Ladder of Jacob described in the vision in which angels ascend and descend. Both the Old and New Testaments abound with astrological lore. Christian ceremonies were borrowed from the Egyptian Gnostics, according to Manly Hall, and from research and observation I would say that is quite evident. He also states in his *PRS Journal* (Winter 1977) that the Gnostic philosophy is divided into Two definite schools—the Syrian and the Greek—and that there is increasing evidence that it gradually centered around the City of Alexandria (Egypt). He also said that most of the hermetic writings first appeared at the same time as the writings of the Sibylline Oracles (not the old, original Sibylline documents).

Oral Scott, in his *The Stars in Myth and Fact,* said that the constellations of the Great Bear and Little Bear circle about the Pole Star and that the Pole Star, since it apparently does not move, represents the consciousness of truth or the understanding and reality of being. He said that when God asked Job if he could guide the Bear's train, he was simply asking if he could control his own mental activities. Scott, in speaking of an American Indian legend, said that lost hunters prayed for guidance and were conducted safely home by the little child who proclaimed herself to be the spirit of the Pole Star. He tells that Hebrew literature suggests a similar idea: "A little child shall lead them." He says further that Jesus taught, "Whosoever shall not receive the Kingdom of God as a little child, shall not enter therein." In other words, innocence and the truth shall make you free. The voice of the higher consciousness within is the small voice giving guidance to that which is right and to all who properly seek it.

CHRISTIAN
Hand posture and halo.

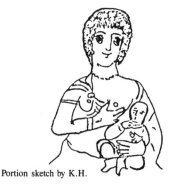

EGYPTIAN
World-Mother
Goddess Isis suckling Horus—resembling
Christian great world mother.

CHRISTIAN
Mother of Jesus suckling the Infant.

CHRISTIAN
Hand posture and halo.
St. Peter's Basilica, Rome

141

Sketch by K.H.

The Paradiso Madonna of Peace
Cloak and halo
Cloaks—symbols of initiation: Blue—spir-
itual; Red—divine love and martyrdom;
Green—gladness of the faithful.
Flow of robes: The power of God and
Universal Energy.

Museum of St. Marco

ASTROLOGIA·XXXVIIII

Astrology, Arts & Science
From Tarocchi Cards (Tarot), Italian. The Cleveland
Museum of Art.

142

Portion sketch by K.H.

CHRISTIAN
St. Mark the Evangelist
Lion (winged), Rooster and Hen, Lion Throne

Portion outline sketch
K.H.

CHRISTIAN
St. Matthew with symbol of the Peacock. Usually shown
with Eagle symbol of the Four Cardinal Points.

143

Portion outline sketch
K.H.

The Christ on a Mandala design with the symbols of the Four Apostles, the Four Cardinal Points of the Zodiac as the Sun passes through, during a year.

Gero Codex, Hessische Landes und Hochschulbibliothek, Darmstadt.

The Christ, in gold relief, with the Twelve Disciples at the Last Supper, and the Sun and Moon by His hand. The Sun is divided into the Four Cardinal Points through which the Sun passes during the year, forming the Cosmic Cross. (Twelve disciples not pictured here.)

Aachen Cathedral

Portion outline sketch
K.H.

144

Portion sketch by K.H.

Christian Madonna with Wheat symbols of Greek Mother Ceres and Moon or Venus crescent. Also symbol of Virgo the Virgin. Ceres, Greek Mother-Goddess, had a daughter Persephone who was taken to the underworld by Pluto.

National Gallery of Art, Washington, D.C.

Twelfth Century Romanesque "Madonna and Child"
of carved, polychromed wood.
Saint Louis Art Museum

Sketch from
wall painting
Portion sketch K.H.

Moses making the water flow from the rock
as did Pegasus smoting the rock on the Mountain in Greek mythology.
Catacomb of St. Callixtus.

Chalice

Grapes:
Egyptian
Greek
Roman
Christian
Jewish

Grapes

Portion sketch by K.H.

JEWISH
Grapes and Chalice
Religious Design

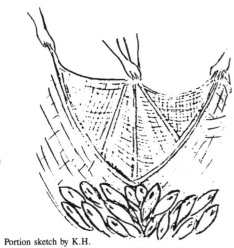

Portion sketch by K.H.
CHRISTIAN
Nets of the Fisher of Men

Portion sketch from "The Holy Family"
oil painting of Jan Gossaert. The infant
Master accepting the Apple or
Pomegranate.
Saint Louis Art Museum

147

Portion sketch by K.H.

Greek Savior Dionysius
Grapes, Fish, Sky Boat like Egyptian.
Found in various art history books.

Portion outline sketch
K.H.

The Ascension of Buddha. Many
Buddhas radiating amid rays of light.

Small section of
the Hell Scroll
Portion outline sketch K.H.

Portion outline sketch
K.H.

Seated Priest with body posture delivering a sermon with Rosary in one
hand and a hand posture with left
hand. Rosary similar to those used
in Catholic faith.

JAPAN
Pictures of these sketches in their en-
tirety are in color in many books on
Oriental Art.

Tokyo National Museum

149

Sketch by K.H.

The Bear is symbolic of a Fixed Star (Sun). The Ram (Lamb) is the Zodiacal symbol of the heavenly constellation Aries. The Bear coincides with the Ladder.

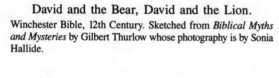

David and the Bear, David and the Lion.
Winchester Bible, 12th Century. Sketched from *Biblical Myths and Mysteries* by Gilbert Thurlow whose photography is by Sonia Hallide.

The Lion is the symbolic power of the Teacher and is also the symbol of the Sun. The Sun passes through the Sign of Aries (the Ram-Lamb) at the time of the Vernal Equinox.

Sketch by K.H.

Outline of symbolic pictures from church windows.

150

Mask from Indians
of Mexico

Arizona State Museum
Sketch of Spider-Turtle Mask

Earth   Air

Water   Fire

Anima Mercurii Fire from the Figuarum
Aegyptiorum.

From *Psychology and Alchemy* by Dr. Carl G. Jung.

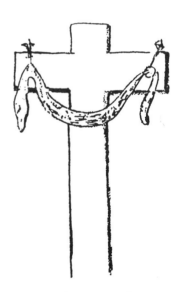

The crucified brazen Serpent
of Moses

From Abraham, *Figures Hieroglifique.*
Sketched from *Psychology and Alchemy* by Dr.
Carl G. Jung.

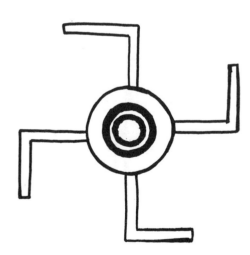

Early Mexican, pre-Columbian
Circle Swastika.

Portion sketches by K.H.

151

Pre-Columbian (Maya),
Greek, Latin, and
Christian Cross.

Oriental Cross,
also Symbol of Venus.
When inverted, a gold orb with the cross
on top is carried by monarchs during
coronation ceremonies.

Gnostic Cross of Egyptian origin.
Fourfold meaning from The Mystery
School.

There are many more forms of crosses
among which are crosses on symbolic
Three steps and columns.

Sketches by K.H.

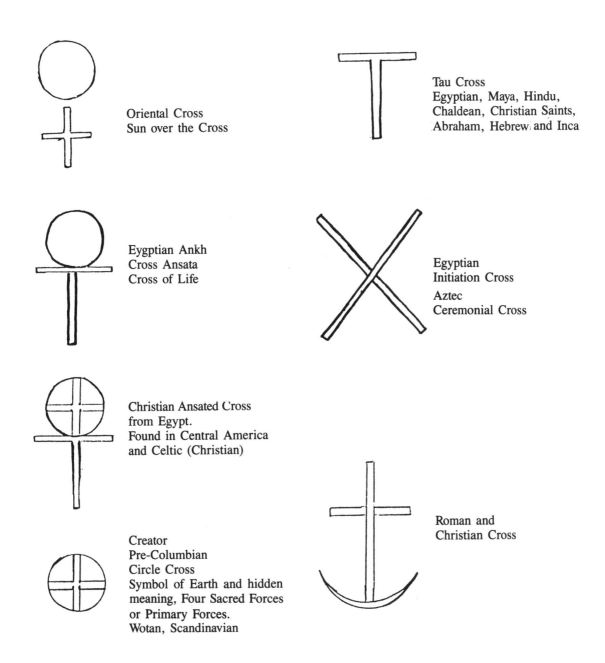

Oriental Cross
Sun over the Cross

Tau Cross
Egyptian, Maya, Hindu,
Chaldean, Christian Saints,
Abraham, Hebrew and Inca

Eygptian Ankh
Cross Ansata
Cross of Life

Egyptian
Initiation Cross
Aztec
Ceremonial Cross

Christian Ansated Cross
from Egypt.
Found in Central America
and Celtic (Christian)

Roman and
Christian Cross

Creator
Pre-Columbian
Circle Cross
Symbol of Earth and hidden
meaning, Four Sacred Forces
or Primary Forces.
Wotan, Scandinavian

Sketches by K.H.

153

JAPAN
Circle Cross Swastika

Swastika—good luck symbol

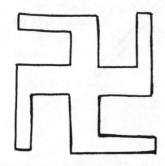

Mexican Cross,
Pre-Columbian
and earlier

Winged Circle
Swastika Cross

**CHINA, JAPAN, AMERICAN INDIAN,
AND PRE-COLUMBIAN**
The Cross in very ancient times represented
Man as a child of the Sun, passing rapidly
through Space, the Solstice and Equinoxes that
form the Cosmic Cross.

The Etruscans had a jagged Swastica
Cross and one of a plain form—
Eighth Century B.C.

From early Circle Cross of
Earth and symbolic of the Sacred Four and the Creator.

154

Cross in Sandpainting
Sandpainting was used by the American Indians
of the Southwest and by the Lamaists of Tibet and
Mongolia.

Philosophical Research Society. From an original drawing by
Hasteen Klah.

Partial sketch
K.H.

Sioux Indian Red Cloud
Feather represents the same idea as the shaved
heads of monks, the single horn (eye) of the Unicorn, the pineal gland, and the Pine Cone.

155

Christian Cross and Hand Posture with the All-Seeing Eye.
Courtesy of the Philosophical Research Society, Inc.

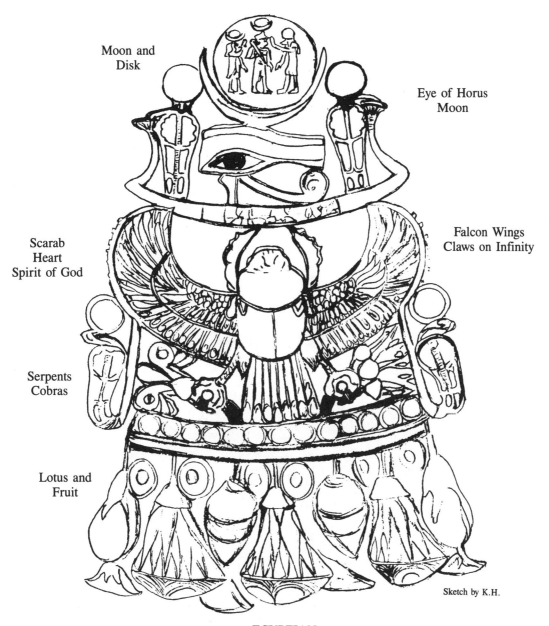

Moon and
Disk

Eye of Horus
Moon

Scarab
Heart
Spirit of God

Falcon Wings
Claws on Infinity

Serpents
Cobras

Lotus and
Fruit

Sketch by K.H.

EGYPTIAN
Symbolic sacred art. Tutankhamon's tomb—chest ornament.

157

Portion sketch by K.H.

Christian Monk. Halo, Vortice in hand.

158

Ladder
Tree
Stones
Angels
River
Birds

Quetzalcoatl of the
Maya descends from
the sky on a Ladder,
also.

Portion sketch by K.H.

Embroidery of Jacob's Dream—Old Testament—early 18th Century English.
Gift of Mrs. Wm. McDonnell to the Saint Louis Art Museum.

Sketch by K.H.

St. John climbs the Lad-
der to heaven.

159

Partial sketch
by K.H.

A Christian Trinity
The Holy Ghost, the Dove, and the Christ
National Gallery of Art, Washington, D.C.

Portion sketch by K.H.

Christian Ladder against the Cross.
From National Gallery of Art, Washington, D.C.

160

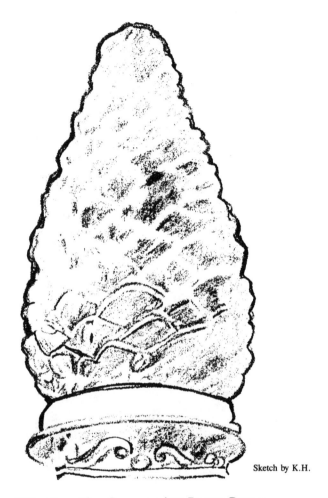

Sketch by K.H.

"Pigna" or Pine Cone—ancient Roman Bronze
Pine Cone symbol for American Indian also; the pineal gland
in the brain (feather symbol), the All-Seeing Eye.

The place found was unknown. Placed in the old St. Peters, moved to
the Court of Belvedere.

161

INDIA
Elephant Deity Ganesha
Philosophical Research Society

HINDU
Multiple heads—Tiger tail
Philosophical Research Society

Stone rubbing of the Chinese Bodhisattva, Kwan Yin, with angel and Lotus flowers.
Philosophical Research Society.

The Japanese Hercules
Allegory as with other Heroes, the Maya Twins, Romulus and Remus, etc.
From an old print, Kathryn Henry Collection.

Sketch by K.H.

ROMAN
A Priestess of Bacchus—altar of
Jupiter—Tree—Serpentine motif.
Victoria and Albert Museum, England

Grapes
Regeneration

Sketch
by K.H.

Michelangelo's Bacchus—Roman
Museum of Bargello, Florence, Italy

GREECE—COIN
Head of Athena and her sacred Owl, a Bird symbolic of
wisdom.

166

The Christ with symbols of Matthew, Mark, Luke and John.

Stained glass window. From the Saint Louis Art Museum. Photographed by the *St. Louis Globe-Democrat.*

Portion sketch by K.H.

167

The Ascension of the Buddha

One of the many Bodhisattvas surrounding Amida Buddha. Lotus decor headdress.

Priest delivering a sermon with rosary.

Found in many books on Japanese art. Photos by Clarke Johnston.

STONES, OTHER ARTIFACTS, SIMILAR PRACTICES AND CHARACTERISTICS COMPARED SCULPTURES, STATUARY, PRINTS, TEMPLES AND PAINTINGS

The language of the Stones is traced through the centuries as a fascinating mystery, the pieces falling into place from time to time with remarkable answers to our questions.

The Emerald Tablet is the Hermetic Stone of Egypt pertaining to the teachings of Hermes. The Rosetta Stone, pyramids and stele have magnificent stories to tell. The double zodiac of the Druid Stonehenge previously mentioned (which is definitely an astronomical/astrological structure) is of great significance. There are the Maya and other pre-Columbian pyramids, monoliths and statuary. There is also a black Stone of the Maya and Hebrews. Strangely, there is also to be found a black Stone in the coronation chair of England and the sacred black Stone of Mecca in Arabia. On the foreheads and headdresses of statuary of different ancient civilizations is the figure of a Cross of one type or another. The Easter Island statuary heads and other stone ruins of many civilizations are treasures that bear much more investigation and consideration than has heretofore been done. Relics of antiquity also bear witness to the widespread use of the Cross.

Significantly identical body postures of ancient statues of deities from the dimly illumined past are the Maya deities and priests and those from the Orient, the Japanese, Chinese and Hindu. Hand postures are important in both Oriental and Christian sacred art. The Hindus call the body postures "manas" and the hand postures "mudras."

Headdresses in all ancient civilizations were indicative of the power of God, and masks had mysterious powers. Spears, scepters and staffs were also magically powerful. All civilizations used them to portray the advancement and evolvement of souls.

Manly Hall said there is a mural from the Codex Troana which has a deity holding a spear and is, according to surviving manuscripts of the Mayas, believed to represent the Hena-god, Votan, of Scandinavia.

The Maya deity and the Buddhist deity both have accentuated earlobes—the Buddhist long, for wisdom and generosity, and the Maya, for the same characteristics, using the round ear plugs of Jade. The thrones of deities of the Maya and Orientals were extremely similar.

There are individuals, deities and angels which are shown with three heads. They are in Celtic, Japanese, Chinese, Hindu, and Christian sacred statues and paintings.

Sketch by K.H.
Brahma
Deity holding rosary; several heads; headdress.
Metropolitan Museum of Art.

Sketch by K.H.

The Christ with hand posture, Three heads and globe with Cross on globe (inverted symbol of Venus).
Volkskunstmuseum, Innsbruck, Austria

Sketch by K.H.

CELTIC
Multiheads
From *The Celtic World* by Barry Cunliffe.

170

Faces from another age look down on the Bayon Temple in the ruins of Angkor. The identical faces, all bearing the same smile, are said to be symbols of Jayavarman VII, last great builder-king of Angkor.

A.P. Photo

Sketch by K.H.

Three-headed Angel by a Hindu sculptor in China or Japan. Found in many books on Japanese art.

STONES

Six tons and nine feet in height with Oriental likeness.

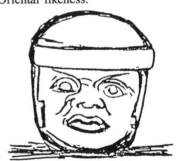

OLMEC (Controversial)
PRE-COLUMBIAN
Could a mother civilization have preceded and left these remnants?

Portion sketch by K.H.

171

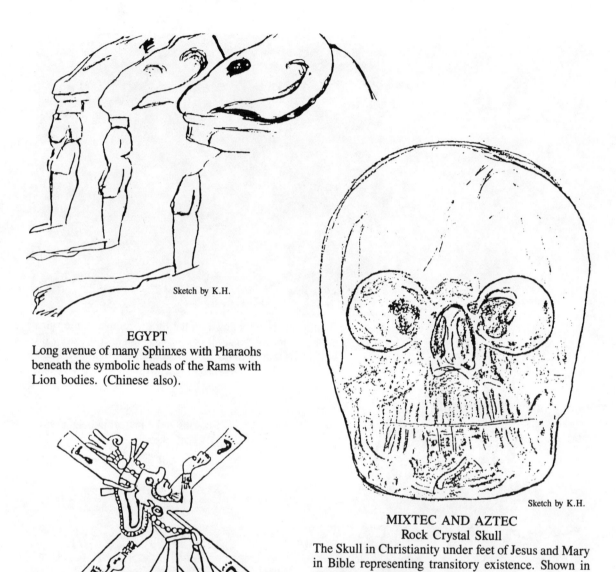

Sketch by K.H.

EGYPT
Long avenue of many Sphinxes with Pharaohs beneath the symbolic heads of the Rams with Lion bodies. (Chinese also).

Portion sketch by K.H.

Sketch by K.H.

MIXTEC AND AZTEC
Rock Crystal Skull
The Skull in Christianity under feet of Jesus and Mary in Bible representing transitory existence. Shown in Catholic sacred art.

British Museum

AZTEC X CROSS
Patron Deity of merchants, but actually more meaningful. The X Cross is on a cloth codex from the Philosophical Research Society. It has the little gold man shooting the golden arrow into the right side of the Aztec crucified Savior on the X Cross (as Egyptian X Cross and Cross of St. Andrew). Liver area, seed atom of lower emotional nature. As Christian Savior and spear.

172

JAPAN
The Buddha
Earlobes

CHINA
The Buddha
Flowing robes

MAYA
Priest head with headdress

Deity
The Lotus—sacred objects

From the collection of Mr. and Mrs. Ed Higgins
Photos by Clarke Johnston

Portion sketch by K.H.

COLOMBIA
Alligator God
(Egypt had one also.)

Portion sketch by K.H.

OLMEC
Deity with Oriental or Mongolian features.

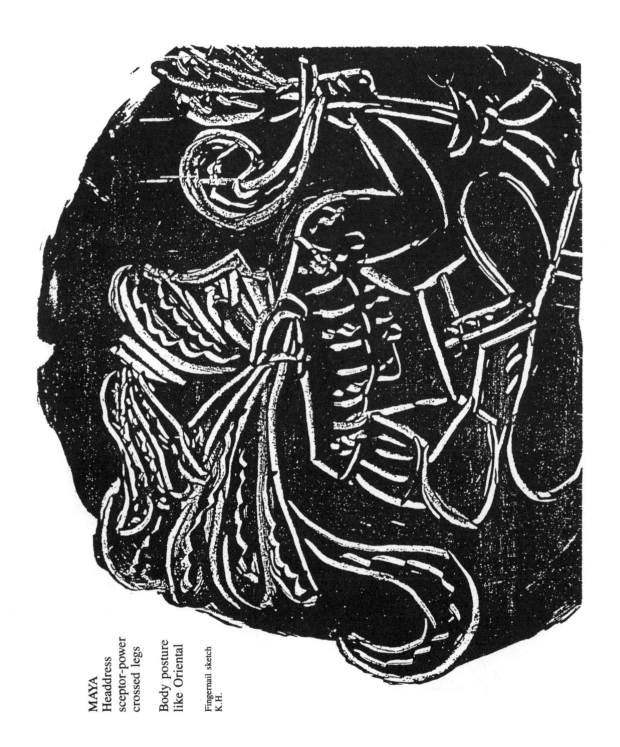

MAYA
Headdress
sceptor-power
crossed legs

Body posture
like Oriental

Fingernail sketch
K.H.

PRE-COLUMBIAN/MAYA
With object similar to double dorje of
the Oriental. Ear plugs.
Photo by Col. Clarke Johnston.

An elaborate silver crown, a ceremonial
covering for the Torah, was loaned to
the Cupples House exhibit by Shaare
Zedek Synagogue.
St. Louis Globe-Democrat Magazine

CHINA
Bodhisattva
From the collection of Mr. and Mrs. Ed Higgins.
Photo by Col. Clarke Johnston.

A Japanese representation of Rahula,
son of Gautama (Buddha), who later became one of the great Arhats of Buddhism.
Philosophical Research Society.
Photo by Abby Kennedy, *Pearls of Wisdom.*

176

JAPAN
Lion Dogs

Shinto Gate
Photos by Harry W. Henry

177

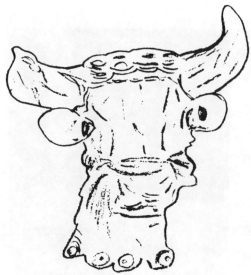

Sketch by K.H.

SUMERIAN
The Bull.
Saint Louis Art Museum

Sketch by K.H.

CHINESE SUNG DYNASTY
Quan Yin
Flowing robes—universal energy.
Saint Louis Art Museum

Sketch by K.H.

EGYPTIAN
Cat, symbol of the universe.

Sketch by K.H.

MAYA
Priest and headdress
National Museum of Mexico

Sketch by K.H.

Gandara Buddha.
A mixture of cultures.
Saint Louis Art Museum

178

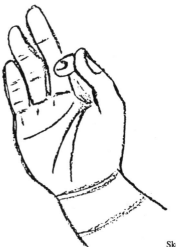

Sketch by K.H.

JAPAN
Hand posture of the Buddha
and bodhisattvas found in
statuary all over the Orient,
similar to Christian.

Portion sketch by K.H.

NEPAL
Deity, male-female.
Hand postures; body posture;
earlobes; headdress.
Asia House Gallery, N.Y.

Portion outline sketch
K.H.

CHINA
Extended hand of Lohan
holding prayer beads. The
figure is dressed in monk's
garments and stands on a
Lotus pedestal.
DeYoung Museum, Avery Bundage
collection.

179

The Buddha

JAPANESE
Amida Buddha and attendants.
Saint Louis Art Museum

JAPAN
Nara
The world's largest bronze statue.

180

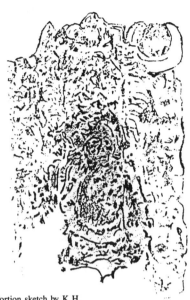

Portion sketch by K.H.

MAYA
Deity on throne (like Oriental style). Cross legged—elaborate throne.

INDIA   Portion sketch by K.H.
Vishnu
Throne resembles those of other Eastern religions and ancient Maya thrones.
Metropolitan Museum of Art

INDIA   Portion sketch by K.H.
Ganesha, elephant symbol, Lord of Lords, center of solar system. Cross-legged body posture.
Metropolitan Museum of Art

181

JAPAN
The Buddha, Chinese base.
Collection of Mr. and Mrs. Robert Brookings
Smith.
Photo by Col. Clarke Johnston

JAPANESE
Bodhisattva of the Moon
Temple at Nara

JAPAN
Kwannon—Goddess of Compassion. It is Quan Yin of China and
Avalokitashvara of India.
Painted by Emily Eversoll.

182

Sketch by K.H.

ITALY
Mercury with Caduceus and wings. Also known as Hermes.
National Museum (Bargello)

Partial sketch by K.H.

TURKEY
Kneeling Angel, Shah Quli, artist. A being on the hat as with Hindu deities on their headdresses.
Smithsonian Institution

Portion sketch by K.H.

EGYPT
A gold statue of Tutankhamon which is completely etched all over with a *feather* design; he carries the Ankh Staff (Cross of Life). He wears a blue helmet. There is a Japanese Deity that is shown in blue color, and Krishna, Deity of India, is colored all in blue. The robes of Mary and Jesus in Christianity are blue, the spiritual color.

183

Portion sketch
by K.H.

INDIA
Vishnu in Fish incarnation.
From *Asiatic Mythology* by Haiken.

Portion sketch by K.H.

Statue of Athena wearing
horned helmet similar to the
Viking, Amerindian, Egyp-
tian, and others. It is said that
in the Christian religion the
Virgin Mary took the place of
Athena and St. George that of
Erechtheus.

Sketch by K.H.

JAPAN
Praying statue—sketched by graves in
Japan for dead children. Hand
posture; earlobes; flowing robes.

Portion outline sketch
K.H.

JAPAN
Goddess Kwannon—compas-
sion. Male-female at one time,
now female. Quan Yin of
China and Avalokitashvara of
the Hindu. Lotus petal base.

184

Deity—Area of Angkor
Brahmanic and Buddhistic in characteristics with conventional form of serpent
on headdress. The large earlobes are
called the "long ears of wisdom."
Carved in the 12th century.
Collection of the Philosophical Research Society.

INDIA
Deity—The Dancing Shiva
The Dance of the Universe

Printed in India

Portion outline sketch
K.H.

Deity Vishnu
Music of the Spheres
Sketched from *Asiatic Mythology* by Haiken

185

MEXICO 600-900 A.D.
The caption says, "Heroic-Seated Female." Deities, all, are both male-
female, having the attributes of power as well as gentility. Even Quan
Yin (China), Kannon (Japan), Avalokitashyara (India), was originally
male-female but because of the element of compassion designated to
that deity, it has more recently been allotted the role of female. Body
posture similar to Oriental. Serpent heads.

Saint Louis Art Museum, Morton D. May Collection
Sketch by Kathryn Henry at Museum

186

Meditating Buddha and Lohans

Lotus pedestal

Buddha on Lotus throne

Aztec Snake goddess

Philosophical Research Society
Photographs by Abby Kennedy

Japan—Deity with Carp—Pearl Eye

Buddha—Lotus Boat—Sea of Life
Philosophical Research Society

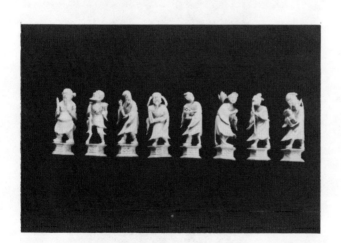

The Eight Immortals—Ivory

BALI
Wooden Owl

Kathryn Henry Collection
Photos by Col. Clarke Johnston

188

Very old statuettes, era unknown. Fish scale legs.
Collection of Marguerite E. Mitchell

THAILAND
Bodhisattva
Earlobes, flowers, headdress. Hand and
body postures—Lotus seat.
Collection of Marguerite E. Mitchell

St. Fiacre, Patron Saint of
Gardens. There are Three
Christian flower symbols.
Woodcarving by Marjorie Maine.
Collection of
Marguerite E. Mitchell

189

Chinese staff and pomegranate, power and advancement.

Chinese Great Teacher Lao-Tse on Water Buffalo.

Photos by Col. Clarke Johnston

INDIA
Sacred tapestry.

Collection of Jane Hunter

JAPAN
Carp—Fish
Sacred symbol as in Christianity.

Maya mosaic by Rae L. Davis
Priest, Headdress and Serpent, Sun and
Birds.

Buddha
Courtesy of Philosophical Research Society.

Tree and Birds

Mountain and Tree

Prints from National Palace Museum, Taipei, Taiwan, from China
Photos by Col. Clarke Johnston

Trees and Mountains

Fowl

Buddha under Bodhi Tree
Philosophical Research Society

Trees and Mountains

Prints from the National Palace Museum, Taipei, Taiwan, Republic of China.
Photos by Col. Clarke Johnston.

Water mural of the Maya from the ruins not yet opened to the public.
Photograph by Ed Higgins.

MAYA
From Kathryn Henry Collection
Photographed by Chandler Kennedy

MAYA
From Kathryn Henry Collection
Photographed by Chandler Kennedy

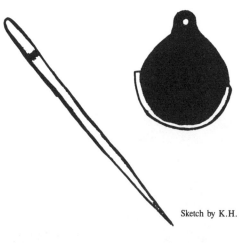

Sketch by K.H.

Obsidian Aztec ceremonial Mirror and Wand. Mirrors used by Japanese (Shinto), Egyptians, Greeks and Romans in sacred ceremonies. The smoking Mirror of prophecy and the symbol of the Goddess Blue Humming Bird.
British Museum

193

JAPAN
Pictures in Temple
Photos by K.H.

The Buddha

Man and Tiger

Deity and Clouds

194

JAPAN
Prayer Lantern and Temple Bells
Photos by K.H.

195

Rubbing by K.H.

Griffin

From an old abbey in England.

STAFFS, LEOPARD SKINS AND SPEARS

Staffs, tridents, spears, and sceptres are all sacred objects of power and advancement—the attainment of the illumined soul which has evolved to untold heights in wisdom and spirituality. It is love-wisdom as in Christianity and the love-wisdom-compassion of the Oriental beliefs.

The Feline species also represents power, universal energy and great forces. It is also representative of deities and Great World Teachers.

197

Sketch K.H.

EGYPT

Mural on wall of Tomb of Tutankhamon-King. Leopard skin. King Ai is performing the rite of opening the mouth of King Tutankhamon, who is shown as Osiris. The Oriental has the Lion—Herakl, Greek (and Hercules, Roman) has the Lion skin, and Maya has the Jaguar.

198

CHINA
Wise Man. Deer-soul. Staff is longevity and power.
Philosophical Research Society, Inc.

SIAM
Staff of power in Lion's paws. Temple rubbing.

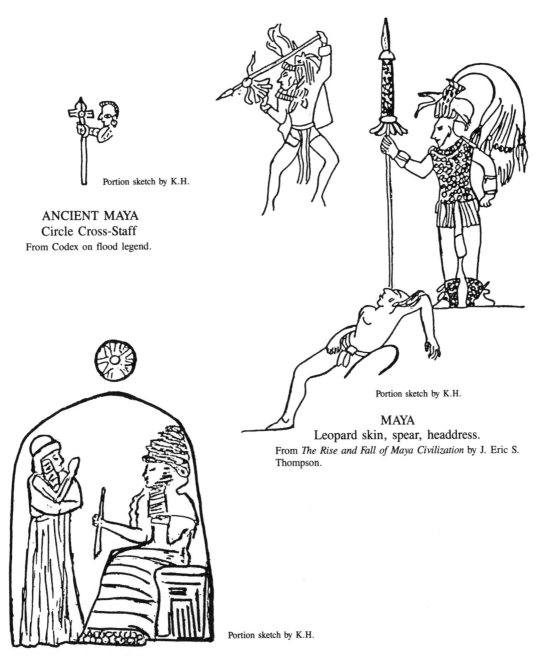

Portion sketch by K.H.

ANCIENT MAYA
Circle Cross-Staff
From Codex on flood legend.

Portion sketch by K.H.

MAYA
Leopard skin, spear, headdress.
From *The Rise and Fall of Maya Civilization* by J. Eric S. Thompson.

Portion sketch by K.H.

BABYLONIAN
Sun God giving the law to the king. Serpent head-dress on the God holding scepter of power.

201

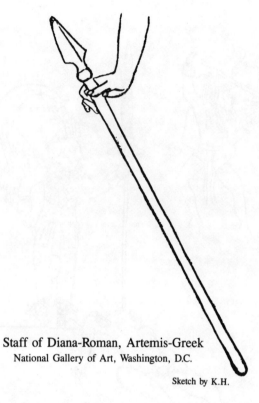

Staff of Diana-Roman, Artemis-Greek
National Gallery of Art, Washington, D.C.

Sketch by K.H.

Portion sketch by K.H.

MAYA, CENTRAL AMERICA
Jaguar

Sketch by K.H.

Diana's Dog, symbol of faithfulness.

Portion sketch by K.H.

ROMAN
Mercury. Winged Hat, Winged Heel and Winged
Escalapian Staff or Caduceus.
National Gallery of Art, Washington, D.C.

202

FRUITS AND DESIGNS

FRUITS

From Robert Graves' *The Greek Myths,* volumes 1 and 2 (Penguin Book Classics), loaned to me by the late Dr. A. H. Compton, we note that he observes that the Greek myths are ingenious theological dogma. He said that the lives of many characters span several generations because these are titles rather than names of particular heroes. He proclaimed that myths, though difficult to reconcile with chronology, are always practical. He said they insist on some point of tradition, however distorted the meaning may have become in the telling. If some myths are baffling at first sight, he believes this is often because the mythographer has accidentally or deliberately misinterpreted a sacred picture or dramatic rite. As an example, Robert Graves tells of the "Apple Myth":

As the story goes, a gift of an apple to Paris from Aphrodite symbolized her love and it was also her passport to the Elysian Fields (which may be the Mystery Schools), called the Apple orchards of the west, to which only the souls of heroes were admitted. He noticed that a similar gift is frequently made in Irish and Welsh myths, as well as by the Three Hesperides to Hercules and by Eve to Adam; that Nemesis, goddess of the sacred grove, who in late myths became a symbol of divine vengeance on proud kings, carried an Apple-hung branch, her gift to heroes. Graves also noticed that Neolithic and Bronze Age paradises were orchard islands, paradise itself meaning "orchard."

Some myths are historical as well as ritual, according to Graves. Manly Hall and others agree. So it seems that the Great World Teachings bestows its love on its advanced souls, the world heroes. There is the myth of Atlanta and the Golden Apples of Greece. The Pomegranate (similar symbol to the Apple) is featured in Japanese, Egyptian, Babylonian, Judaic, and Christian symbolic sacred art. In both sculpturing and painting, deities are shown holding sacred objects. Describing the garments of the high priest of Judaism, the Book of Exodus, chapter 28, reads that the garments of the high priest, Aaron, are blue, purple and scarlet with Pomegranates decorating them.

Many authors have written about the mysteries and sacred ceremonies. Manly Hall said of the mystery schools that when corruption entered the mysteries, a division occurred, and some of the secrets fell into the hands of the profane (masses) who perverted them, as in the case of the Bacchanalia, during which, he says, drugs were mixed with wine and became the real cause of the orgies, which were definitely not representative of the standards of purity of the mysteries. The Bacchic was of a very high order, but later degraded.

In the Egyptian, Greek and Christian practices, the Grape stood for regeneration and spiritual ecstasy, the Christians taking this from the Egyptian ceremonies. Grapes were used in religious art and the wine from the Grapes in religious ceremonies.

There is an Egyptian frieze belonging to the Saint Louis Art Museum with the Grapes, the Vines and the Bird; Greek friezes show only the Grapes and Vines.

Jesus said, "I am the Vine," and according to Manly Hall, Bacchic and Christian rites are linked together by use of the monogram "IHS" (sacred name); their purpose was to disentangle the rational from the irrational soul. Bacchus also was identified with Jesus by the surname Panther (feline).

Bacchic rites were superseded by the Mithric rites of the Persians and were called the Titian monad by Pythagoras, the great Greek philosopher-mathematician. Mr. Hall said the ancients held Bacchus as the form of solar energy, having the attributes of the Sun; he was the higher nature of man, the crucified Savior and his resurrection. Dionysius is the same as Bacchus in ancient Greek mythology, and Dionysius was called the Vine god. In the Bacchic and Dionysian mysteries, they were the gods of ecstasy, and the Grape and the Vine were the symbols of divine ecstasy.

There is a statue of Dionysius with Grapes in his hair, and the Bacchanti wave wands bound round with leaves and tendrils of the Vine, the living Vine whose life in them was the soul of ecstasy, and the Grape equalling spiritual transformation.

Divine energy is the true Christian communion cup, and in the Bible it states that "He who drinks it (divine energy—wine) remembers his troubles no more," as with St. Francis and Noah who were "drunk" with the ecstasy of God. They were not drunk from overindulgence of an alcoholic beverage, as this author once heard a minister complain about to a graduating class. He said, "Wasn't it terrible that Noah got drunk?"!

Manly Hall said that we learn that the Dervishes and Sufis of Islam had their cups and winebibbing religious ceremonies, too, and the Sufis claimed to be "intoxicated with God," and from Omar, "Forgetfulness that rests in the Vine." The Grape (and Vine) are symbols of universal consciousness, and religious ecstasy is realizing the universal (the whole of life of the world) and the human soul's approach to the divine. He shows an old Roman engraving or print of Saturn swallowing a large Stone (substituted for Jupiter) and being surrounded by Grape Vines.

Bacchus is also compared to the Hindu crucified Savior, Christna. In Egypt, Isis has a bunch of Grapes on the right breast, and on the left is corn or wheat (gold) which is Sunlight, spiritual gold, the first sperm of life, which Manly Hall says is the spiritual fire of nature that "does all and is all in all." Plato told of the Christos myth of which Bacchus was a form; there is also a relation here between Christos, Bacchus and Jesus and the Holy Grail.

Catholic churches all over the world have Grapes, Leaves and Vines in their decor, and a Protestant church has the Grape symbol on the rostrum (in St. Louis, Missouri). George Ferguson, in his book, *Signs and Symbols in Christian Art,* describes the wine press as being a symbol of God's wrath.

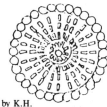

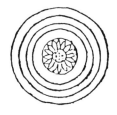

Portion sketch by K.H.

CAMBODIA
Daisy in the center of Sun Circle. Found on Seven-headed Serpent.

Sketch by K.H.

ANCIENT HINDU
Winged Circle

Sketch by K.H.

MAYA
Winged Circle

Sketch by K.H.

MOORISH-SPANISH
Portion of design—Serpentine

Portion sketch by K.H.

Viking design, similar to Chinese.
Rough sketch

205

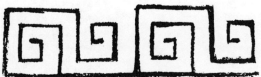

Sketch by K.H.

Japanese Design
Similar to Greek key.

Portion sketch by K.H.

Greek design on cup. Peleus and Thetis, Greek key
design, Lion and Serpents.

From *Athenian Red Figure Vases, The Archaic Period* by John
Broadman.

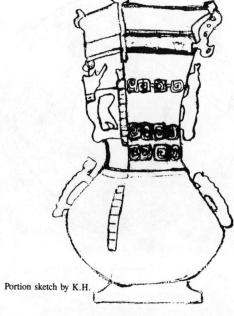

Portion sketch by K.H.

Chinese Vessel
Scroll is similar to Maya and
Nordic design.

206

Infant with Halo

Portion sketch by K.H.

Mother and Hindu infant deity (left)
Infant deity on Mt. Govardhan—
body posture under tree (right)

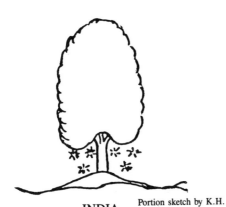

Portion sketch by K.H.

INDIA
Sacred Kadamba Tree
On Mount Govardhan

Portion sketch by K.H.

INDIA
Bird design
India God-Krishna
Peacock-Crown-Halo (on tur-
ban), long earlobes.

207

Portion sketch by K.H.

INDIA
Tree, Palm fan, Peacock fan, Birds, Bulls, Fish, and Flowers
Portion of ceremonial spiritual print.

208

INDIA

The Sun, Plantain leaves and
Chariots of the Gods drawn by Bull
and Swan.

Portions of ceremonial spiritual prints.

INDIA

Egret Birds, Fish, Lotus

Portions of sacred paintings

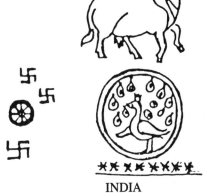

INDIA

Symbols from portions of sacred
paintings. Swastika Cross, Peacock
Bird and Stars, Cow—Taurus,
Zodiacal. Once leader of Zodiac,
4,000 years ago.

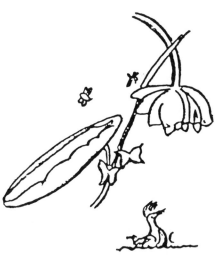

INDIA

The Bee, the Lotus flower, Butterflies,
and the Egret Bird.

Portions of sacred paintings.

INDIA

Phoenix—Sacred mythological bird

Rubbing from brass plate collection of Kathryn
Henry.

Portion sketches by K.H.

209

ENGLAND
Interlaced design from Winchester Bible.

FRANCE
Serpent head. Interlaced Bible design.

ITALY
Interlacing bands in design used by Raphael and other great artists. Found in churches and Bibles. All similar to ancient Celtic work in Ireland. "There is nothing new under the Sun."

CHRISTIAN
Grapes
"I am the Vine"

SCANDINAVIAN
Design on little wooden casket. Resembles Celts, Maya and Chinese.

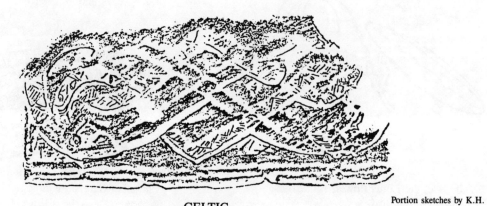

Portion sketches by K.H.

CELTIC
Serpentine motif interlaced (like Maya decor and others).

EGYPTIAN
Falcon

EGYPT
Bee—one of the symbols of Egypt.
I suspect deeper meanings as well
and as with others.

Vulture

Cobra

Sedge

Portion Sketches by K.H.

211

PRE-COLUMBIAN
Similar to Greek key design.

Top of Wall
Rounded corners on straight lines (like circle and square) giving balance of male-female, positive and negative, gives unique Maya decor in paintings and architecture.

Forces coming from mouths of animals.
From Palace of Atetelco, Atetitla, Central America. Palace being renovated, never opened to public. Pictures from the collection of Alvine Higgin.

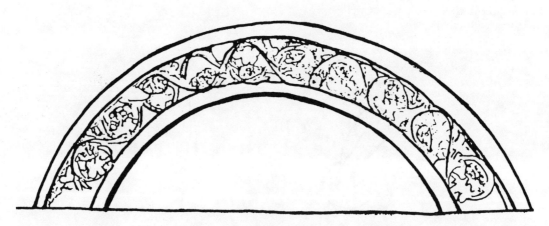

ITALIAN
Grape Vine design on interior entrance of church.

Portion sketches by K.H.

212

FRUITS AND DESIGNS

JUDAISM

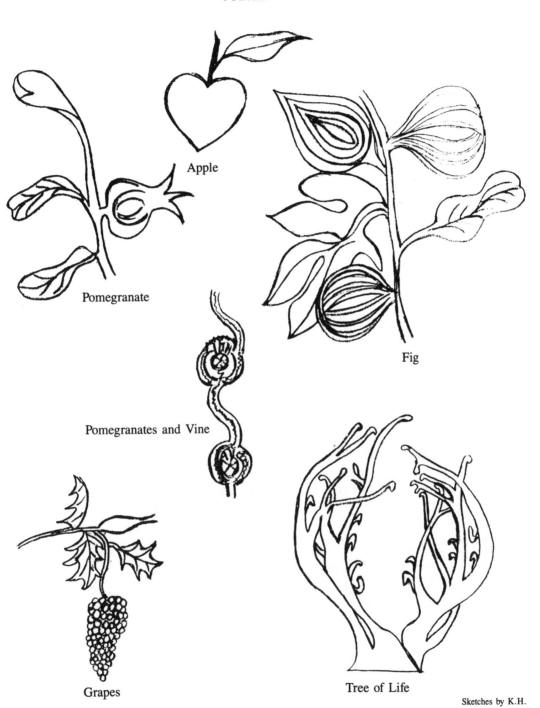

Apple

Pomegranate

Fig

Pomegranates and Vine

Grapes

Tree of Life

Sketches by K.H.

213

JUDAISM

Peacock

Conjoined Horns
forming heart shape

Double-headed Phoenix Bird
(mythological)

ISRAELITE
Horned Altar

Dove

Mandala
Portion of mosaic floor. Mandalas are found in many ancient civilizations as a sacred focal point for meditation.

Sketches by K.H.

214

MAYA
Secton of Mask

AMERICAN INDIAN
Southeast portion of
copper plaque with eye
in palm of hand as in
Christian and others.

CHINA
Shang period. Section
of Jaguar mask, simi-
lar to Greek key.

MAYA
Feathered Serpent Deity.
British Museum after Mauds-
lay, similar to Chinese and
others, hand posture similar to
Oriental and Christian. Can be
found in *The Civilizations of
the Maya*, Chicago Natural
History Museum Press.

BRAZIL
Portion of design on
funery urn similar to
China and Maya.

CHINA
On bronze vessel,
Shang period.

AMERICAN INDIAN
Turtle, Southwest. Similar to
Greek key.

JAVA
A Makara, similar to East
Indian and others.

VALLEY OF MEXICO
Similar to Greek key.

All these examples (except the Feathered Serpent) can be found in *The Eagle, The Jaguar, and the
Serpent* by Miguel Covarrubias.

Sketches by K.H.

215

NUMBERS, SOME ZODIACAL SYMBOLS AND MANDALAS

NUMBERS

There is numerical symbolism in many ancient civilizations and particularly in the Cabala of the ancient Hebrew in which are featured many geometric forms, cubes, diagrams, stars with numbered points, and calculus and trigonometry involving astrology. In ancient times astrology was the mother science while astronomy was the very small, physical part of it. The Cabala was composed of higher mathematics as was that which surrounded the mysteries of the Pyramid of Gizeh and the Pyramid mysteries of the ancient Maya of Central America and others. The number Three played a prominent part in ancient religions in the form of Trinities. Astrology, with its higher mathematics, was extremely important in all ancient civilizations and was used by millions of people for thousands of years in their religions and philosophies.

We will concentrate mainly on the numbers Seven, Four and Twelve at this time. There are the Seven original planets displayed in all cultures of antiquity, the Seven layers of the earth, the Seven continents, the Seven seas, the Seven days of the week, and the Seven layers of skin.

In the Bible there are the Seven letters and seals in St. John (Revelations), the Seven books, Seven angels, Seven vials, Seven trumpets, Seven stars in God's Hand (Seven angels or planets), Seven churches, Seven candlesticks (Jewish and Christian), Seven veils, Seven lamps of fire, Seven spirits of God, the Seven lines, and the Seven plagues. There are Seven ventricles in the brain and Seven chambers in the heart.

There are the Seven tests of initiation (planetary) for the twins of the Xibalban mysteries of the ancient Maya. In Christianity we find a Seven-headed Serpent. There is also the Seven-headed Greek Serpent. In Hinduism, we discover that the red serpent, Kundalini, coils at the base of the spine and ascends the human spine, touching off the Seven chakras as man evolves. These are ruled by the Seven original planets. The Seven sacred Cows and Bulls of Egypt are very meaningful. There are the Seven kings of Rome as well.

In India, there are the Seven ways to bliss and in Egypt, the Seven inexorable powers, the Seven Hebrew vowels, the Seven lives (according to Helena Petrovna Blavatsky), the Seven eternities (eons), and the Seven horses. There are also the Seven sisters of the Pleiades, a star group. In the more recent fairy tale allegory of "Snow White," there are Seven dwarfs.

Robert Graves said that Zeus bears bursts of the Seven Planetary Powers on his shield and that when the Titan cult was abolished in Greece and the Seven-day week ceased to figure in the official calendar, their number was quoted as Twelve by some authors, probably to make them correspond with the signs of the zodiac. (This is Germanic also, which the Celts borrowed from the Eastern Mediterranean.) It also took Seven years to build Solomon's Temple, according to the Biblical allegory.

There is a mythological Batman who participates in one of the Seven tests of the Maya twins in the Xibalban mysteries of Central America (the Seven original planets), as previously mentioned. The Bat in China is a symbol of happiness, differing here from the frightening Bat of the Maya which eventually will lead to happiness through tested soul development.

The Seventh labor of Hercules concerns the Cretan Bull. There are the Seven lucky gods of Japan and the Seven virtues of the Rose Croix of Egyptian Freemasonry:

1. Patience
2. Moderation
3. Temperance
4. Modesty
5. Prudence
6. Mildness
7. Candor

As to the Four fixed astrological signs and symbols of Matthew, Mark, Luke, and John and the vision of Ezekiel, Aquarius is the face of the angel (human), Taurus the face of the Ox (Bull), Scorpio the face of the Eagle (Serpent and Dove), and Leo the face of the Lion. These Four are also sometimes pictured as the Bull (Taurus) with a human face, the human form—Aquarius, the Lion with the man's head—Leo, the Eagle head—Scorpio. The Four Primary Forces are associated with the Four colors, the Four directions on the globe, the Four gods, Four geniuses, Four Genii, and the Four Pillars. There are the Four winds, the Four corners of the earth and the Four elements (earth, fire, air, and water) and the Fourth hall of learning.

The Chinese book, *Tchi*, 18,000 years ago recorded the Twelve dynasties of kings. Japan has from antiquity recorded the same Twelve dynasties, an ancient Hindu manuscript tells of the Twelve dynasties of kings, and the Maya (Central America) of Chicken Itza inscription also tells of the Twelve dynasties. Egyptian priest-historians on scribe written papyri mentioned the reign of another great and much earlier ancient civilization, preceding theirs, of Twelve islands. The Twelve Sibyls were active in the early Bronze Age and on into the later Greek and Roman civilizations. Michelangelo of Rome painted the Erythrean Sibyl in the Sistine Chapel. Manly Hall writes of the Twelve Sibyls in various books and particularly in his quarterly *PRS Journal* (Winter 1977). In mythology of antiquity there is a Tree of Life bearing Twelve fruits and every year giving fruit for Twelve months. (In antiquity, the Twelve signs of the zodiac in connection with wisdom and knowledge were directly related to evolvement through time-space.) There are the Twelve journeys of the Greek Odysseus (Ulysses in Roman mythology), the Twelve tribes of Israel, the Twelve knights of the Round Table, the Twelve disciples of Christ, and the Twelve tasks of Herakles (Greek), Hercules (Roman).

MANDALAS

The center of a Mandala is where the power is located as is energy from the Sun in a solar system, like the nucleus and peripheral of an egg or a cell. Great stone circle Mandalas on the ground were executed by ancient peoples in different parts of the world, in various civilizations and in different time eras. These were the microcosms of the macrocosm of our solar system. They were the opposite polarities of the heavenly bodies. They were the above to the below. They were powerful and sacred with mysterious overtones. This is true of the small personal Mandalas also, but in a different way. They are used as a point of concentration during meditation with deep connotations.

The stained glass window in the Cathedral at Chartres in France is a beautiful Mandala of the western Christian type, like the Oriental rose medallion. In Stonehenge of the Druids there were 300 or more such circles covering the British Isles and more still over on the Continent.

Great cosmic stone circles have been found on the ground in Iran. The rotation of Venus was traced and timed in Yucatan by the Maya. In Australia the natives worshipped the beneficent Fixed Star called Sirius (Dog Star) and had their stone star maps on the ground. The pyramid of Gizeh in Egypt was built mathematically in relation to the sunrise and the sunset. They watched the sky in India from turreted circled structures and in Persia from the ziggurat towers.

John Mitchell, in his *The Secret of the Stones,* wrote about Alfred Watkins, a Britisher who discovered the "ley system." Peter Tompkins also wrote about him in *Mysteries of the Mexican Pyramids*. Alfred Watkins discovered in 1922 the honeycombed stone system underground and covering the earth. He believed, as do others, that this system is electromagnetic and that the ancients built various structures on the cross-sections of this system—the Pyramid of Gizeh having been built on a cross-section. In 1925 he published a book on these lines called *The Old Straight Track*. It is also said that the Cathedral at Chartres was built over a mound that was erected on one of the ley system cross points. The circles and lines correspond as opposite polarities to the heavenly bodies.

In his *The Earth Spirit,* John Mitchell tells of the energy (electromagnetic power) that came from an enormous rock in Australia which sustained the natives in an otherwise desert area.

Two women have written books on gems that are of great interest. Both have Ph.D.s in geology and are gemologists. Thelma Isaacs, in *Gemstones, Crystals and Healing,* tells of the electronic forces in gems that are emitted when properly treated and especially of the tremendous energy coming from rock crystals. The American Indians still heal with crystals.

In *The Healing Stones,* Doris Hodges tells how Catherine of Aragon's ruby ring paled drastically in color before she was made to divorce Henry VIII. She mentions that methane can be released from garnets.

In *The Celtic Druids* by Godfrey Higgins (preface by Manly P. Hall), Higgins tells of a circular stone temple of the Greeks having no statue or image in it that was built to Zeus (Jupiter) on a Mountaintop. All ancient civilizations had mysterious great stones.

219

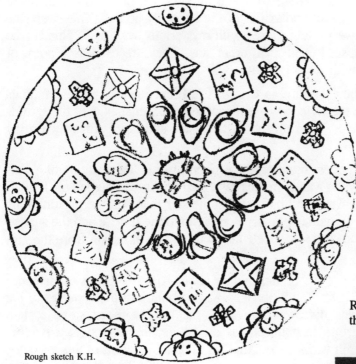

Rough sketch K.H.

FRANCE
Rose Mandala stained glass window in
the Cathedral at Chartres.

Photo by H. W. Henry

220

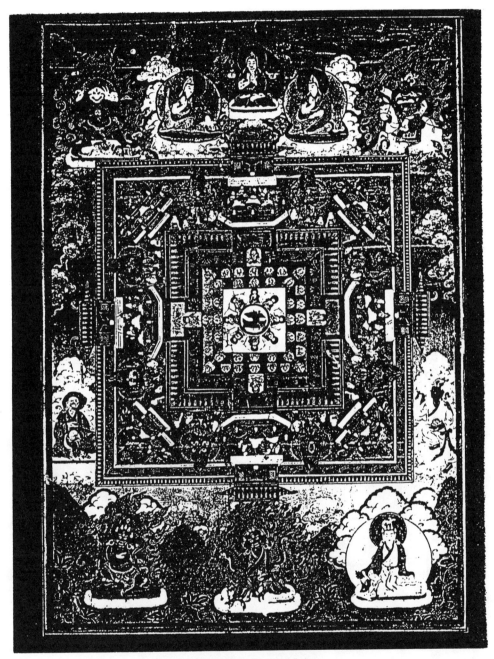

TIBETAN MANDALA
Philosophical Research Society, Inc.

CHINESE ZODIAC
Twelve House Signs

EGYPTIAN ZODIAC

God has the sickle to reap the harvest, and the angel uses the sickle to reap the grapes of regeneration. The sickle is Time. Similar to Druids.

Sketch from Rudolph Steiner's God Man who appeared to St. John in Revelation. He has the sword in his mouth which brings light to earth and sets men free. Here are the Seven original planets and the Twelve signs of the zodiac. Paul and Daniel spoke of astrology in the Bible. Paul spoke of the Christ Consciousness within as Socrates did of the Daimon, the Buddhic Consciousness and the Nam of the Hindu.

Portion sketch of Albrecht Dürer's woodcut of the Son of Man or the God Man of John's vision in Revelation. It has the Sun's rays, the Seven original planets in his hand and the sword in his mouth; he is surrounded by the Seven candlesticks.

Portion sketches by K.H.

224

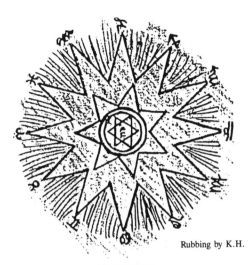

Rubbing by K.H.

HEBREW
Circle Sunburst of Zodiac

The Moon Mounds of Shells were used by the ancient Hebrews in sacred ceremonies. In *The Greek Myths* by Robert Graves, he speaks of their mounds representing the Sun and Moon, built of sea shells, quartz and white marble. The Sun was subordinate to the Moon until later Greek myths.

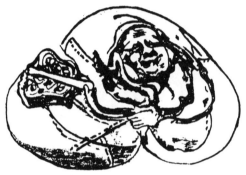

Sketch by K.H.

JAPAN

The Seven Gods of Luck appeared to Hotei in a dream. The Seven original planets: In Christianity, in the vision (dream) of St. John, there were the Seven lamps of fire which are the Seven spirits of God and the Seven points of light through which the One Holy Spirit is revealed. Other Sevens have been mentioned elsewhere in the book, but the Seven colors of the Rainbow must be added.

Metropolitan Museum of Art

Sketch by K.H.

Venus, inverted

Carried by rulers Greek, Roman and Britain.

225

THE ZODIAC

These sketch outlines of mosaics were designed from the Astrological
Zodiac by Raphael and executed by Luigi de Pace of Venice.

Chigi Chapel, Romo, Santa Marie del Popolo

The Crab and Moon are on the head of
Diana. The foot leaving may symbolize
things reversing. King Lear said, "With
the Crab ascending, all the affairs of my
life go backwards."

Venus rules both Libra, the scales,
and Taurus, the Bull.

Diana, Goddess of the Moon and the
Hunt (for wisdom). The Moon rules the
Mother, the home, the masses, and there
are other key words.

Apollo, the Sun God, has the Sun on his
head, which rules the sign of Leo, symbolized by the power of the Lion.

Mars rules both Aries, the Ram (Lamb)
and the sign of Scorpio, the Scorpion.
Sometimes the Serpent, Eagle and Dove
are depicted as the Three types of the
Scorpio sign. Some key words are
death, war, science, music, etc.

Partial sketch outlines by K.H.

226

Venus on Fish with Lion's head
From engraving by Agostino Veneziano

Sketch outline of the throne of Pope Leo
X as Clement I. Giuilo Romano, a pupil
of Raphael, shows him between two
statues, Temperance and Meekness,
with the signs of the Zodiac encircling
the top of the throne. Visible are the
signs Taurus the Bull, Gemini the
Twins, Cancer the Crab, Leo the Lion,
Virgo the Virgin, Libra the Scales, and
Scorpio the Scorpion.

The Vatican

Partial sketches by K.H.

子 丑 寅 卯 辰 巳 午 未 申 酉 戌 亥

JAPANESE ZODIAC
Ivory, Metropolitan Museum of Art

Sketch by K.H.

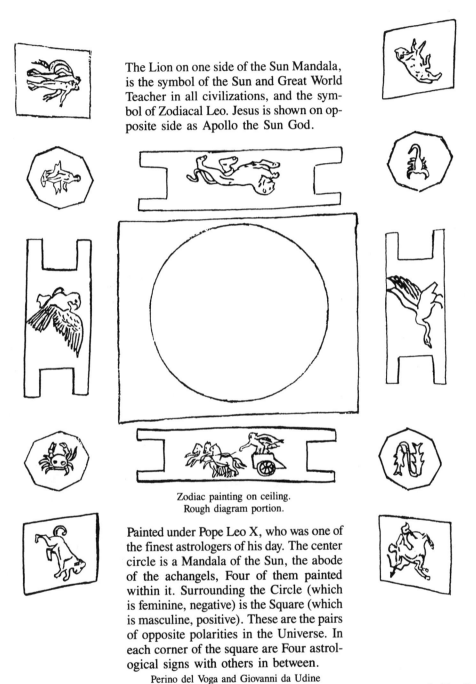

The Lion on one side of the Sun Mandala, is the symbol of the Sun and Great World Teacher in all civilizations, and the symbol of Zodiacal Leo. Jesus is shown on opposite side as Apollo the Sun God.

Zodiac painting on ceiling.
Rough diagram portion.

Painted under Pope Leo X, who was one of the finest astrologers of his day. The center circle is a Mandala of the Sun, the abode of the achangels, Four of them painted within it. Surrounding the Circle (which is feminine, negative) is the Square (which is masculine, positive). These are the pairs of opposite polarities in the Universe. In each corner of the square are Four astrological signs with others in between.

Perino del Voga and Giovanni da Udine
Borgia Apartment, The Vatican

Partial outline sketch
by K.H.

229

CAVES

From Manly P. Hall's *America's Assignment with Destiny,* I quote: "Unprejudiced observers have been forced to conclude that among most tribes of Amerinds (American Indians) magical rituals are performed involving the use of natural forces beyond the normal experience of human beings. (See *Some Strange Corners of our Country* by Charles F. Summis.) The Amerindic concept of cosmogony paralleled, in a general way, that of the Chaldeans and other people who dwelt in the valley of the Euphrates. The world consisted of three regions, with human beings inhabiting the surface of the central zone. Above this middle land was an airy expanse extending to the abode of the Sky-Father. Below the surface were subterranean levels extending downward to the place of the earth-mother. This cavernous region was like the dark and shadowy underworld of the Pre-Homeric Greeks."

The Japanese and ancient Maya of Central America also had their Caves and underground zones of religious and sacred connotations. In Japan, it is the Cave of the Sun Goddess. In the American Indian, it is the Cave of the Spider Woman, as mentioned in the Ladder chapter. In Greece, the Oracles pronounced from Caves as did the Maya prophetesses in Central America.

JAPAN COMPARED

There is drum beating in Japanese ritual, as with India where the drum of Shiva is the heartbeat and pulse of the Universe. The American Indian, Haitians and Africans also use drums. The Japanese have Kuzudi dancing, Bells, Mirror (Shinto), Sun goddess, and the Sword for severing the spiritual from the material world (also in India). The Moon plays a prominent part as well as the Sun in their sacred rituals. The Rope or Cord in Japanese Shinto faith is also used by Christian monks in symbolism, and both use rosary beads. One of the Cord meanings is "happiness, forever."

Thousands upon thousands of symbolic examples could be given, and we've touched on just the surface of the subject. The study of symbolism is as inexhaustible as the study of the celestial dome of the heavens. Universal law and its symbols are for all life and time, throughout space.

OTHER CHARACTERISTICS COMPARED

Maggie Wilson, in her article in *Arizona Highways* magazine, tells of geographic features such as Mountains that are combined with supernatural or deified entities and events of this kind associated with the beliefs of the North American Indian. The Mountain in many ancient religions is, as mentioned before, identified with the head, the most energized part of the physical body, and the heart wherein the spirit of God resides. This is taught to the followers of several religions and philosophies in the world.

One tribe of Amerindians has a maze legend, as with the Greek mythology, of the labyrinth which was guarded by the Minotaur. The Lion-dogs of Fu guard the temple and soul in the Orient, which is a similarity as we've mentioned under mythological animals. These symbols stand for the overcoming of obstacles on the road of life in the testing of character for soul development.

The Indians recognized the nature spirits, symbolized by the Kachina dolls, just as the people of Ireland recognized the "little people." The Pueblo Indians were also aware of the Solstices and Equinoxes as were the Indians of Cahokia in 1100 B.C. who were thriving at that time in Illinois near St. Louis, Missouri. At the Machu Picchu ruins of the Incas in Peru, South America, at the Temple of the Sun, there is a circular building (observatory) with stone pegs surrounding the windows which were used to secure a sighting device for determining the Solar Equinox. The Inca Empire was larger than the Roman Empire, but short-lived (*Washington University Magazine,* Fall 1984, St. Louis, Missouri). In the ruins of the ancient Maya of Central America, there are observatories, as with the Druids (British Isles) and all over the Celtic areas. Many tribes, cultures and civilizations recognized the great cosmic occurrences of the heavens and followed them. We must not forget the marvels of the Pyramid of Gizeh of Egypt, which some believe was built by a mother civilization long before the Egyptian people became a civilization.

ADDITIONAL SYMBOLISM
ACCORDING TO MANLY HALL

There are those who are fascinated with the richness, the intrigue and the depth of the magic that lies behind symbol sacred art. This work is for all mankind, having been gathered from the ancients who were very select and who executed these miraculous, mysterious and very meaningful objects.

Just as the writing of this material was concluded, Manly Palmer Hall, in his Winter 1985 *PRS Journal,* wrote several articles pertaining to symbolism. I will give the gist here since his research pertains vitally to this book.

Where Trees are sacred symbols, he speaks of various Trees—the Fate Tree or the Life Tree of Athena, which was the life and light of the city of Athens and of the Greek people; the Tree of the Hesperides, which was guarded by a Serpent and bore golden Fruit, and sometimes planets and metals were found growing on the branches of the Tree of Knowledge. For thousands of years the Serpent has been a symbol of wisdom, and Jesus admonished his followers to be as wise as Serpents. "Moses raised a golden serpent in the wilderness for the salvation of his people as indicated in the Old Testament. It is also prominent in alchemy and the hermetic arts and throughout the world it is highly venerated as a symbol of wisdom."

Further, according to Manly Hall, "Because snakes are believed to live in subterranean openings in the earth, they were associated with the initiatory rites (of The Mystery Schools) which were usually performed in caves, grottos or subterranean chambers beneath temples or tombs."

In the life of the Buddha, he described that Buddha was born under a Tree in the Lumbini Gardens, received enlightenment under the sacred Banyan Tree or Bodhi Tree, preached his first sermon seated under a Tree at Sarnath, and died in a grove of Sala Trees.

Another sacred writing giving veneration for Trees is in the *Book of Revelation,* chapter 22, verse 2. John writes: "In the midst of the street of it and on either side of the river *was there* the tree of life, bore twelve manner of fruits *and* yielded her fruit every month: and the leaves of the trees *were* for the healing of nations."

Mr. Hall goes on to say that the Tree is a Christian symbol. The winter Solstice was deeply involved in astro-theology, and the Evergreen came to be regarded as a symbol of immortality because it survived the rigors of winter. He tells of the Scandinavians as far back as the Eighth Century A.D. attaching a pine Tree to the ridgepole of a building being erected. (This custom is a prevalent ceremony today!)

He continues on to say that in Asiatic countries the pine Tree was associated with good fortune and a promise of immortality. "The only decoration on the back wall of the Japanese

Noh Theater was a pine Tree. As the Noh plays were decidedly religious, the Tree design could be interpreted as a blessing or as a symbol of the presence of the Shinto deities. The use of the pine as a fortunate emblem was widely diffused among ancient peoples and may have reached Europe from Asia or the Near East."

Mr. Hall notes that in the Japanese calendar the pine Tree was directly associated with the winter Solstice. It is the central attraction in their gardens and bonzai art. "The medicinal value of the pine tree was discovered long ago and was regarded as remedial for a number of ailments, especially those affecting the respiratory system. This tree has very few enemies and is not subject to infestation or accidental decay. It heals its own wounds." Mr. Hall reminds us that the Tree gives us so much. It shows us that "ALL comes from ONE and in the course of time returns to the ONE."

He said that the cat-goddess, Bast, of Egypt is depicted wearing a cobra on her head, and that although occasionally identified with the Lion, Bast was basically a protectress.

These are only a minute few of the great many about which he has researched and written.

SYMBOLISM OF FAMOUS WORKS

Amazingly, the following unusual masterpieces are extremely symbolic and were created with a deliberate purpose. Unfortunately, there is a limit as to how much can be written about them here, to give a full explanation for each of these wonderful adventures.

Mozart's *Magic Flute*
The Wizard of Oz by L. Frank Baum
The Ring of the Nielbelung by Richard Wagner
Sinbad the Sailor
The Shakespearean plays, which had double meanings
Dante's *Divine Comedy*
Alice in Wonderland by Lewis Carroll

It would take the writing of another book in order to go into the magnificent symbolism of each of these great works for man to penetrate. There are books written on the symbolism of color (one by L. Bayley) and also on the symbolism of geometric forms and of gems.

This story now ends, but there is no ending to the story of symbolism.

BIBLIOGRAPHIC REFERENCES

Aldred, Cyril. *Akhenaten*. New York: McGraw-Hill Book Company, 1968.

Allen, Judy and Griffiths, Jeanne. *The Book of the Dragon*. Chartwell Books, Inc., 1979.

Amos, H.D. and Long, A.G.P. *These Were the Greeks*. Dufour Editions, Inc., 1979.

Ancient Egypt. New York Times, Inc., 1965.

Anthony, Ilid E. *Roman London*. G. P. Putnam's Sons, 1971.

Anton, Ferdinand. *Art of the Maya*. G. P. Putnam's Sons, 1970.

Arguelles, Jose and Mirian. *Mandala*. Shambhala, 1972.

Backes, Magnus and Dolling, Regine. *Art of the Dark Ages*. New York: Harry N. Abrams, Inc. Publishers, 1969.

Baley, Harold. *The Lost Language of Symbolism* (Vols. I, II). London and Tonbridge: Ernest Benn Limited. New Jersey: Rowman and Littlefield Limited, 1951. (First published by Williams and Norgate, Ltd., 1912.)

Beltran, Orlando A. *Symbolism of Oriental Religious Art*. The Philosophical Research Society, 1953.

Blavatsky, H. P. *The Secret Doctrine*, 1888. Los Angeles: The Theosophical Company, 1925.

Bloch, Raymond. *The Ancient Civilization of the Etruscans (An Archeological Adventure)*. Geneva, Switzerland: Nagel Publishers, 1969.

Boardman, John. *Athenian Black Figure Vases*. Oxford University Press, 1974.

Boardman, John. *Athenian Red Figure Vase*. The Archaic Period. Oxford University Press, 1975.

Boardman, John. *Greek Art* (Revised edition). Oxford University Press, 1973.

Boas, Franz. *Primitive Art*. New York: Dover Publications, Inc., 1955.

The Book of Job. William Blake (1757-1827) (illustrator), Michael Marquesee (new introduction). Two Continents Publishing Group, 1976.

Bowra, C. M. *Classical Greece*. Time Incorporated, 1965.

Breasted, J. H. *Development of Religion and Thought in Ancient Egypt*. Harper & Brothers Publishers, 1959.

Brown, Peter. *The World of Late Antiquity*. Thames and Hudson, 1971.

Bryner, Edna. *Thirteen Tibetan Tankas*. The Falcon's Wing Press, 1956.

Budge, Sir E. A. Wallis. *The Egyptian Book of The Dead*. New York: Dover Publications, Inc., 1967.

Budge, Sir E. A. Wallis. *Egyptian Magic*. New Hyde Park: University Books, 1899.

Budge, Sir E. A. Wallis. *Tutankhamen*. New York: Bell Publishing Co., 1923.

Burland, Cottie. *North American Indian Mythology*. Paul Hamlyn Limited, 1965.

Burling, Judith and Hart, Arthur. *Chinese Art*. Viking Press, 1953.

Bussagli, Mario (Professor, University of Rome) and Sivaramamurti, Calembus (Director, The National Museum of New Delhi). *5,000 Years of the Art of India* (no date given).

Butsch, Albert Fidelis. *Handbook of Renaissance Ornament*. New York: Dover Publications, Inc., 1969.

Calvesi, Maurizio. *Treasures of the Vatican.* Horizon Magazine, 1962.

Campbell, Joseph. *The Hero with a Thousand Faces.* Princeton University Press, 1949.

Campbell, Joseph. *The Masks of God (Occidental Mythology).* Viking Press, 1964.

Campbell, Joseph. *The Masks of God (Oriental Mythology).* Viking Press, 1962.

Casson, L., Claiborne, R., Fagan, B., and Karb, W. *Mysteries of the Past.* American Heritage Publishing Company, 1977.

Ceram, C. W. *Gods, Graves and Scholars.* New York: Alfred Knopf, 1976.

Ceram, C. W. *Hands on the Past.* Alfred A. Knopf, 1966.

Ceram, C. W. *The Secrets of the Hittites.* Alfred A. Knopf, Inc., 1955.

Cervantes, Maria Antonieta. *Treasures of Ancient Mexico.* From The National Anthropological Museum. 2nd ed. New York: Crescent Books, 1978.

Chiba, Reiko. *The Seven Lucky Gods of Japan.* Charles E. Tuttle Company, 1966.

Chiera, Edward. *They Wrote on Clay.* Chicago: The University of Chicago Press, 1938.

The Chinese Exhibition, the Exhibition of Archaeological Finds of the People's Republic of China. Nelson Gallery Foundation, 1975.

Clark, R. T. Rundle. *Myth and Symbol in Ancient Egypt.* Thames and Hudson, 1959.

The Complete Works of Raphael. New York: Harrison House Publishers, 1969.

Covarrubios, Miguel. *The Eagle, the Jaguar, and the Serpent.* Alfred A. Knopf, 1954.

Cristofani, Mauro. *The Etruscans.* Galahad Books, 1978.

Daniel, Glyn. *The Minoans—The Story of the Bronze Age.* New York: Praeger Publishers, 1971.

Dannaud, J. P. *Cambodge.* Lausanne, Switzerland: La Guilde du Livre, 1959.

De Garis, Frederic. *We Japanese.* Yomagata Press, 1934.

Delsol, Paula. *Chinese Horoscopes.* Pan, 1969.

de Lubicz. *Her-Bak, Egyptian Initiate.* New York: Inner Traditions International Ltd., 1967.

Deneck, M. M. *Indian Art.* Octopus Books, 1972.

De Silva-Vigier, Anil. *The Life of the Buddha.* Phaidon Press, 1955.

Edwards, I. E. S. *Tutankhamun, His Tomb and Its Treasures.* New York: The Metropolitan Museum of Art and Alfred A. Knopf, Inc., 1977.

Egypt—Paintings from Tombs and Temples. (Mohamed Naguib, Preface and Jacques Vandier, Introduction). New York: The New York Graphic Society by arangement with UNESCO, 1954.

"Egyptian Museum, Cairo." *Great Museums of the World.* New York: Newsweek/Mondadori, 1969.

Ekram. *Art of the World—The Art of Greece.* Akurgal, 1966.

Encyclopedia of World Mythology. (Warner, Rex, Foreword). Galahad Books, 1975.

Evans-Wentz, W. Y. (compiled and ed.). *The Tibetan Book of the Dead.* Oxford University Press, 1927.

Fend, Gia-Fu and English, Jane. *Lao Tsu Tao Te Ching.* Vintage Books, Random House, 1979.

Ferguson, George. *Signs and Symbols in Christian Art.* New York: A Galaxy Book, Oxford University Press, 1966.

Ferandez, Justine. *Mexican Art—The Colour Library of Art.* London, New York, Sydney,

242

Toronto: Paul Hamlyn (no date given).

Feuchtwagner, Franz. *The Art of Ancient Mexico.* Thames and Hudson, 1954.

Field, D. M. *Greek and Roman Mythology.* Chartwell Books, Inc. The Hamlyn Publishing Group Limited, 1977.

Forman, W. and Barinka, J. *The Art of Ancient Korea.* London: Peter Nevill, Ltd., Westbrook House, 1962.

Frazer, James George, Sir. *The Golden Bough.* The Macmillan Company, 1922.

Gardener, Helen, *Art through the Ages.* New York: Harcourt, Brace & Co., 1926.

Gita, Kim and Murray, Chris. *Illuminations from the Bhagavad-Gita.* Harper & Row Publishers, 1972.

Goetz, Delia and Morley, Sylvanus G. (English version). *Popol Vah, The Sacred Book of the Ancient Quiche Maya.* The University of Oklahoma Press, 1950.

Graham, Lloyd M. *Deceptions and Myths of the Bible.* Bell Publishing Company, 1979.

Graves, Robert. *The Greek Myths* (Vols. I, II). Penguin Books, 1955.

Graves, Robert. *The White Goddess.* Vintage Books, Inc. (reprint, Farrar Straus & Cudahy, Inc.), 1948.

Grimm's Fairy Tales. (Elenore Abbott, selected and illustrated). Charles Scribners Sons, 1920.

Haiken, J. *Asiatic Mythology.* New York: Crescent Books, Crowell Publishing Co., 1963.

Hale, John R. and the Editors of Time-Life Books. *Great Ages of Man (Renaissance).* 1965.

Hall, Manly P. *Codex Rosae Crucis.* The Philosophical Research Society, Inc., 1971.

Hall, Manly P. *Freemasonry of the Ancient Egyptians.* The Philosophical Research Society, Inc., 1937.

Hall, Manly P. *Healing, The Divine Art.* The Philosophical Research Society, Inc., 1943.

Hall, Manly P. *Lectures on Ancient Philosophy.* The Philosophical Research Society, Inc., 1929.

Hall, Manly P. *The Lost Keys of Freemasonry or the Secret of Hiram Abiff.* Macoy Publishing and Masonic Supply Company, 1923.

Hall, Manly P. *Man, The Grand Symbol of the Mysteries.* The Philosophical Research Society, Inc. 1932.

Hall, Manly P. *The Secret Teachings of All Ages.* The Philosophical Research Society, Inc., 1962.

Hall, Manly P. *The Story of Astrology.* The Philosophical Research Society, 1975.

Hall, Manly P. *Twelve World Teachers.* The Philosophical Research Society, Inc., 1947.

Hammond, N. G. L. and Scullard, H. H. *The Oxford Classical Dictionary.* 1970.

Heline, Corinne. *Esoteric Music, Based on the Musical Seership of Richard Wagner.* New Age Press, 1948.

Heline, Corinne. *Mystic Masonry and the Bible.*, New Age Press, 1963.

Heline, Corinne. *The Twelve Labors of Hercules.* New Age Press, Inc., 1944.

Higgins, Godfrey, Esq. *The Celtic Druids.* The Philosophical Research Society, Inc., 1977. Originally published, 1829.

Hillier, J. *Hokusai.* Phaidon Publishers, Inc., 1955.

Hitchcock, Ethan Allen. *The Red Book of Appin,* 1866. The Philosophical Research Society, Inc., 1977.

Hogarth, Peter and Clery, Val. *Dragons.* The Viking Press, 1979.

Holloway, R. Ross. *A View of Greek Art.* Brown University Press, 1973.

Holme, Bryan and Campbell, Joseph. *Bulfinch's Mythology—The Greek and Roman Fables Illustrated.* The Viking Press, 1979.

The Holy Bible.

Hood, Sinclair. The Minoans—The Story of Bronze Age Crete. Praeger Publishers, 1971.

The Horizon Book of Lost Worlds. American Heritage Publishing Co., Inc., 1962.

Huyghe, Rene (Ed.). *Larousse Encyclopedia of Mythology.* (Robert Graves, introduction). New York: Paul Hamlyn Limited, Prometheus Press, 1959.

Huyghe, Rene (Ed.). *Larousse Encyclopedia of Prehistoric Ancient Art: Art and Mankind.* New York: Prometheus Press, 1967.

The Iliad of Homer. Lattimore, Richmond, 1957.

Imperial Rome. Time-Life Books, Inc., 1965.

India—Paintings from Ajanta Caves. (Nehru, Jawaharlal, Preface and Singh, Mahanjeet, Introduction). New York: The New York Graphic Society by arrangement with UNESCO, 1954.

Indian Art—The Color Library of Art. Paul Hamlyn Limited, 1967.

Irie, et. al. *Masterpieces of Japanese Sculpture.* Bijutsu Shuppan-Sha and Charles E. Tuttle Co., 1961.

Jacobs, Jolande (Ed.). *Paracelsus.* Bollingen Series XXVIII, Princeton University Press, 1942.

Janson, H. W. and Cauman, Samuel. *A Basic History of Art.* Prentice-Hall, Inc., Harry N. Abrams, Inc., 1971.

Japan—Ancient Buddhist Paintings. (Elisseeff, Serge, Preface and Matsushita, Takaaki, Introduction). New York: The New York Graphic Society by arrangement with UNESCO, 1959.

Japanese Paintings. Mentor-Unesco Art Book. New York: The New American Library of World Literature, Inc., 1963.

Journey Into China. Washington, D.C.: National Geographic Society, 1982.

Jung, Carl G. *Man and His Symbols.* Doubleday and Company, 1964.

Jung, C. G. *Psychology and Alchemy.* Bollingen Foundation, Inc. New York: Pantheon Books, 1953.

Kitto, H.D.F. *The Greeks.* A Pelican Book. Great Britain: Penguin Books, C. Nichalls and Company, Ltd., 1951.

Koch, Rudolf. *The Book of Signs.* Dover Publications, Inc., 1955.

Lamy, Lucie. *Egyptian Mysteries.* New York: Crossroad, 1981.

Lauf, Detlef Ingo. *Tibetan Sacred Art (The Heritage of Tantra).* Shambala Publications, Inc., 1976.

Lenzini, Margherita and Miceletti, Emma. *Masterpieces of Painting in the Uffizi Gallery.* 1971.

244

Leonard, Jonathan Norton and the Editors of Time-Life Books. *Ancient America.* 1967.

Lewinsohn, Richard. *Animals, Men and Myths.* Harper and Brothers, 1954.

Lewis, Bernard (Ed.). *Islam and the Arab World.* Alfred A. Knopf, American Heritage Publishing Company, Inc., 1976.

The Light of the Past, A Treasury of Horizon. American Heritage Publishing Co., 1959.

Lullies, R. and Hirmer, M. *Greek Sculpture.* Harry N. Abrams, Inc., 1957.

Lum, Peter. *Fabulous Beast.* Thames and Hudson, 1952.

Luzzatto-Blitz, Oscar. *Antique Jade.* Paul Hamlyn Limited, 1969.

MacKenzie, Finlay. *Chinese Art.* Paul Hamlyn Limited, 1961.

Mallakh, Kamal El with Bianchi, Robert. *Treasures of the Nile.* Tokyo: Newsweek, Inc. and Kodansha Ltd., 1980.

Mansuelli, Guido. *Art of the World.* Crown Publishers, 1965.

Masterpieces of Chinese Painting. National Palace Museum, 1969.

Mexico—Pre-Hispanic Paintings. (Soustelle, Jacques, Preface and Bernal, Ignacio, Introduction). New York: The New York Graphic Society by arrangement with UNESCO, 1958.

Miller, Madeleine S. and Lane, J. *The New Harper's Bible Dictionary.* Harper and Row Publishers, 1952.

Moor, Edward. *Hindu Pantheon.* Los Angeles: Philosophical Research Society, 1976.

Morley, Sylvanus G. *The Ancient Maya.* Stanford, Ca.: Stanford University Press, 1946.

Munsterberg, Hugo. *The Arts of China.* Rutland, Vermont: Charles E. Tuttle Company, 1972.

Murray, Kim and Chris. *Illuminations from the Bhagavad-Gita.* Harper and Row, 1980.

Narazaki, Muneshige. *Masterworks of Ukiyo—E Studies in Nature—Hokusai-Hiroshige.* (John Bester, trans.) Kodansha International, Ltd., 1970.

"National Museum of Anthropology—Mexico City," *Great Museums of the World.* Newsweek/Simon and Schuster, 1970.

Nesbitt, Alexander. *Decorative Alphabets and Initials.* Dover Publications, Inc., 1959.

Nivedita, Sister (Margaret E. Noble). *Cradle Tales of Hinduism.* 3rd impression. Vedanta Press, 1975.

Norton-Taylor, Duncan and the Editors of Time-Life Books. *The Celts, the Emergence of Man.* 1974.

Olcott, William Tyler. *Sun Lore of All Ages.* G. P. Putnam's Sons, 1914.

Otto, Walter F. *The Homeric Gods.* Pantheon, 1954.

Oxenstierna, Eric. *The Norsemen.* New York: New York Graphic Society Publishers, Ltd., 1965.

Pagels, Elaine. *The Gnostic Gospels.* Random House, 1979.

Paintings from Pompeii, Herculaneum and Stabia. The Museum Nationale at Naples, 1964.

Palmer, J. P. *Jade.* Spring Books, Paul Hamlyn Ltd., 1967.

Parsons, Lee A. *Pre-Columbian Art—The Morton D. May and The Saint Louis Art Museum Collections.* Harper and Row Publishers, 1980.

Patrick, Richard. *All Color Book of Egyptian Mythology.* 1972.

Patrick, Richard. *Egyptian Mythology.* (Margaret Drower, Introduction). New York: Crescent Books. (First English edition published by Octopus Books Limited, 1972.)

Proddow, Penelope. *Art Tells a Story—Greek and Roman Myths.* Doubleday Publications, 1979.

Purce, Jill. *The Mystic Spiral (Journey of the Soul).* Avon Books, 1974.

Quispel, Gilles. *The Secret Book of Revelation,* 1979.

Raine, Kathleen and Harper, G. M. (edited with introductions). *Thomas Taylor, The Platonist (Includes Iamblicus).* Bollingen Series, Princeton University Press, 1969.

Raphaelian, H. M. *Signs of Life. A Pictorial Dictionary of Symbols.* Anatol Sivas Publication, 1957.

Rebel in the Soul. (Bika Reed, translation and commentary). Inner Traditions International, 1978.

Rivet, Paul. *Maya Cities.* New York: G. P. Putnam's Sons, 1960.

Roberts, Moss (Ed. and trans.). *Chinese Fairy Tales and Fantasies.* New York: Pantheon Books, 1979.

Robertson, Martin, et al. *Greek Painting.* Rozzoli International Publications, Inc., 1979.

Robinson, Herbert Spencer and Wilson, Knox. *Myths and Legends of All Nations.* Doubleday and Company, 1950.

Rowland, Benjamin. *The Ajanta Caves.* Mentor-Unesco Art Book. New York: The New American Library of World Literature, Inc., 1963.

Sagara, Tokuzo. *Japanese Fine Arts.* Tokyo: Japan Travel Bureau, 1949.

Scholem, Gershom. *On the Kabbalalah and Its Symbolism.* Ralph Manheim (Trans.). New York: Schocken Books, Inc., 1965.

Schrader, J.S. *A Medieval Bestiary.* The Metropolitan Museum of Art (summer bulletin), 1986.

Schuchhardt, C. *Schliemann's Discoveries of the Ancient World.* Avenel Books, 1979.

Scott, Oral E. *The Stars in Myth and Fact.* The Caxton Printers, Ltd., 1942.

Seligmann, Kurt. *The History of Magic.* Pantheon Books, Inc., 1948.

Skira, Albert (planned and directed collection). *Egyptian Painting, The Great Centuries of Painting.* Geneva, Paris, New York: 1954.

Smart, Ninian. *The Long Search.* Little, Brown and Company, 1977.

Stacey-Judd, Robert B. *Atlantis—Mother of Empires.* Devorss and Company, 1939.

Stenico, Arturo (University of Milan). *Roman and Etruscan Painting.* (Andre Held and D. W. Bloemena, Eds.) The Viking Press, 1963.

Stern, Harold P. *Birds, Beasts, Blossoms, and Bugs.* Harry N. Abrams, Inc. Publishers, 1976.

Taylor, Thomas. *Iamblicus and The Mysteries.* Chiswick, England: 1821.

Thompson, J. Eric S. *The Civilization of the Mayas.* Chicago: Chicago Natural History Museum Press, 1927.

Thompson, J. Eric S. *The Rise and Fall of Maya Civilization.* University of Oklahoma Press, 1954.

Thurlow, Gilbert. *Biblical Myths and Mysteries.* Octopus Books Limited, 1974.

Time Line of Culture in the Nile Valley and Its Relationship to Other World Cultures. The Metropolitan Museum of Art (bulletin).

Tompkins, Peter. *Mystery of the Mexican Pyramids.* New York: Harper & Row Publishers, 1976.

Tompkins, Peter. *Secrets of the Great Pyramid.* New York: Harper & Row Publishers, 1971.

Treasures of Britain. W. W. Norton and Co., Inc., 1968. (First American edition, 1969).

Tsuda, Noritake. *Handbook of Japanese Art.* Tokyo: Sanseido Company, 1941. Charles E. Tuttle Company, 1976.

Turnbull, Coulson. *The Solar Logos.* The Gnostic Press, 1923.

Vermeule, Emily. *Greece in the Bronze Age.* University of Chicago Press, 1964.

von Franz, Marie-Louise. *Time, Rhythm and Repose.* Thames and Hudson Publishers, 1978.

Waite, Arthur Edward. *The Hermetic and Alchemical Writings of Paracelsus* (Vols. I, II). 1894.

Waite, Arthur Edward. *A New Encyclopedia of Freemasonry.* Weathervane Books, 1970.

Warner, Rex (Foreword). *Encyclopedia of World Mythology.* 3rd ed. New York: Galahad Books, 1975.

Waters, Frank. *Book of the Hopi.* An Intext Publication, 1963.

Watson, William. *Ancient China—The Discoveries of Post Liberation Archaeology.* New York Graphic Society, 1974.

Weigel, James, Jr. *Mythology.* Cliffs Notes, Inc., 1973.

West, John Anthony. *Serpent in the Sky: The High Wisdom of Ancient Egypt.* New York: Harper & Row Publishers, 1979.

Westcott, W. Wynn, M.B. *The Isiac Tablet or the Bembine Table of Isis.* The Philosophical Research Society, 1976.

Wheeler, Sir Morton (introduction). *Pompeii and Herculaneum.* London: Spring Books; Drury House, 1966.

White, Anne Terry. *The American Indian.* (John F. Kennedy, Introduction). Random House, 1963.

White, Anne Terry. *The Golden Treasury of Myths and Legends.* New York: Golden Press, 1959.

White, T. H. *The Bestiary, a Book of Beasts.* G. P. Putnam's Sons, Capricorn Books Editions, 1960.

Williams, C. A. S. *Outlines of Chinese Symbolism and Art Motives.* Charles E. Tuttle Company, 1974.

Woldering, Irmgard. *The Art of Egypt.* Grey Stone Press, 1963.

The World of Classical Athens. Florence, Italy: Bemporal Marzocco, 1966; Macdonald & Co. (Publishers) Ltd., 1970.

The World's Great Religions. Time-Life, Inc., 1957.

The World's Last Mysteries, The Reader's Digest Association, Limited, 1976.

Yap, Yong and Cotterell, Arthur. *The Early Civilization of China.* G. P. Putnam's Sons, 1975.

Yashiro, Yukio. *2,000 Years of Japanese Art.* Harry N. Abrams, Inc., 1958.

Yvon Rene. *Chinese Treasures from the Avery Brundage Collection.* Lefebvre d'Argencé Asia House Gallery Publications, 1968.